It's Going to Be All Right

Arthur A. Milward

It's Going to Be All Right

REVIEW AND HERALD® PUBLISHING ASSOCIATION
Since 1861 | www.reviewandherald.com

Published by Review and Herald® Publishing Association, Hagerstown, MD 21741-1119

Review and Herald® titles may be purchased in bulk for educational, business, fund-raising, or sales promotional use. For information, please e-mail SpecialMarkets@reviewandherald.com.

The Review and Herald® Publishing Association publishes biblically based materials for spiritual, physical, and mental growth and Christian discipleship.

The author assumes full responsibility for the accuracy of all facts and quotations as cited in this book.

Unless otherwise indicated, Bible texts are from the King James Version.

Scripture quotations marked NLT are taken from the *Holy Bible,* New Living Translation, copyright © 1996, 2004, 2007. Used by permission of Tyndale House Publishers, Inc., Carol Stream, Illinois 60188. All rights reserved.

This book was
Edited by Lori Peckham
Copyedited by Jeremy J. Johnson
Designed by Review and Herald Design Center
Cover art by Steve Crietz
Typeset: Bembo 12/15

PRINTED IN U.S.A.
16   15   14   13   12   5   4   3   2   1

Library of Congress Cataloging-in-Publication Data
Milward, Arthur A., 1923-2009.
  It's going to be all right : more true stories of / Arthur A. Milward.
    p. cm.
  Includes bibliographical references and index.
  1. Christian life—Seventh-Day Adventist authors. 2. Milward, Arthur A., 1923-2009. I. Title.
  BV4515.3.M59 2012
  286.7092—dc23
  [B]
                              2011040465
ISBN 978-0-8280-2563-8

Acknowledgments

Special thanks goes to Arthur Milward's daughters, Vicki Sammons and Veronica Crockett, who facilitated the completion of this book after their father's death on October 28, 2009.—The editor.

Contents

Introduction

"Out of the Strong Came Forth Sweetness"
—Judges 14:14

Samson—his love life and his propensity for riddles—has often given me pause for thought. And long ago I arrived at the conclusion that for the analogy to be truly meaningful, the message of this anecdote had to be, not the potential strength or power of the late-lamented king of beasts, but its current condition: dead, worthless—indeed, offensive, stinking, and repellent.

Samson's "actual" experience, real or imaginary, conveys to me a message that out of a totally revolting, negative situation can come, by the grace of God, a sweet, nourishing, altogether positive and even beautiful result. How many times throughout my relatively long life has this been made clear to me? Too many to enumerate.

But let me begin at the very beginning. Obviously I do not recall the very first incidence that illustrates this concept, although certainly I was present on the occasion. I was born at my home on the edge of the moors in Derbyshire, England, on October 26, 1923, at which time, I have learned, a blizzard was in progress.

The details of my entry into the world, my making my appearance on the stage—as William Shakespeare has it, to "play my part"—are, naturally, hearsay. However, I had those details provided to me a good deal later by several of those present. They are, I believe, authentic and reliable.

I made my debut, so to speak, somewhat earlier than anticipated, being born a couple of months prematurely, weighing in at a little less than three pounds.

The cast of characters anticipating, eagerly or not, my "arrival" involved, inevitably, my mother, the attending physician, a midwife, my father, and the woman selected to be my nanny, in case that responsibility would turn out to be necessary.

Evidently, it would seem, my mother and I were equally anxious to part company, as it were.

"Take it away," demanded my mother. "I need to rest."

(As the conversation was repeated to me verbatim later, I attempted to interpret her demand as an unawareness of the sex of her offspring, nothing more.)

My father, a country man, eyed whatever "it" was held in the hands of the doctor and, examining me somewhat distastefully, observed: "He [at least he got that right] looks like a skinned rabbit."

The doctor, eyeing me professionally, made his pronouncement. "I really don't think he will live," he assured anyone who was interested. The midwife, by this time, had cared for her duties of attending to my person.

To the point, my prospective nanny, who had so far remained silent, sprang into action, vociferously and with a vengeance. She came forward, seized me from the astonished doctor's hands, crying out, "Give him to me. He's going to live. I won't let him die."

Wrapping a shawl around my tiny body, she ran with me in her hands through several rooms to the warm nursery, previously prepared for my arrival, and proceeded to dedicate the next several years of her life to fulfilling her promise: "I won't let him die." And she didn't.

During the next several years, throughout my "growing up" period, she nurtured and loved me, physically and emotionally. I would never have survived without her, physically, psychologically, or emotionally. She was there for me then and on so very many occasions when I desperately needed someone—and she was that someone.

On countless occasions (by the grace of my heavenly Father, who saw something worth salvaging, who brought sweetness, solace, and encouragement in times of almost unbearable grief, horror, and despair) this has been the pattern of my life.

How can I forget Nanny Fearn, the sweet woman who dedicated her life to loving and caring for other people's children, and who was there for me and found me lovable . . . every day of her life.

My little big sister, Mary, who called me "Boo" (she was only 17 months my senior), on countless occasions "put me back together" when I "fell apart." As I grew into a hypersensitive, often tearful young boy, she never ridiculed me or criticized me for my "weakness." With perception way beyond her tender years, she would often initially remain silent on one of these not infrequent occasions. She would just take me in her arms and hold me. Then, when I had calmed down a bit, she would pull out the hanky all little girls hid in a "secret" pocket stitched to their underwear in those days, "mop me up," and whisper in my ear, "I love you, Boo."

As I grew, there were other occasions: Notably, during my service in World War II, observing firsthand "man's inhumanity to man" in its unbelievable horror, there were incidents that reassured me that "all was not lost," that there was still beauty, even love, in a world gone mad.

It was mostly the children: The little boy, ragged, thin, and dirty, at the end of the "fighting" war, one of the many roaming the highways and byways of Europe seeking parents from whom they had been separated. Clutching his little piece of crumpled paper in his small hand, he would approach any passing serviceman and accost him:

"Excuse, please, Herr Officer. Have you seen this man? He is my father." His father's name was written on the paper.

The inevitable response had to be: "Sorry, sonny, I haven't seen him." And the grieving child—once again—turned away and continued his search.

The horror was there; tragedy was there. And so was the beauty—the triumph of the child's love for his parent, his persistence in his potentially fruitless search for the object of his love. The spark of "divinity" in the human spirit still survived.

How many, old and young, are currently searching desperately for a Father who, maybe, they have lost or perhaps have never really known.

Later my marriage ended, but I still had my beloved children, whose unending love and devotion have sustained me these many years.

Some time previous, when my precious firstborn little boy, Adrian (Ady), was spending the final few months of his life in a London hospital and I visited him daily, knowing it would not be for long, the interaction I was able to have with him and the other children, all in a similar situation, proved an incredible, life-affirming contrast to the "realities" of our situation.

How can I forget the children, Ady's wardmates, who came to me after he had settled in for the night and confided to me their hopes, their fears, their beliefs? There was Sheila, who knew: "I expect I shall have wings."

There was Carolyn, who "didn't want to die," who "wanted to live and to love and be loved."

There was Jeremy, who loved the little girl in a bed across from his. He prayed: "God, help Stephanie. She has these seizures, and it scares her. She's hurting, God. She's just a kid, God. Oh, God, don't let her hurt anymore. Let me hurt instead of her."

And my own little son, not quite 4 years old, who did his best to comfort me. He patted my hand, ever so gently, and encouraged me: "Don't cry, little Daddy."

And finally, when it came time to say "goodbye" to him—for now—he asked me, not for an explanation or a reason, but for assurance only: "Daddy, is it going to be all right?"

I asked my closest companion, who has always accompanied me from my earliest years. I asked the sweet Spirit, "What shall I say? What can I tell him?" And the answer came.

"Ady, sweetheart," I said, "don't be afraid. It is going to be all right."

He smiled at me, gave a big sigh, and closed his eyes and went to sleep.

He believed me. He knew it would be all right, because Daddy said so.

The Father tells me that He will "give unto them beauty for ashes, the oil of joy for mourning, the garment of praise for the spirit of heaviness" (Isaiah 61:3), and the sweet, fragrant taste of the honeycomb.

Chapter 1

The Mysterious Tombstone

Oddly enough, one of the favorite pastimes of my sister, Mary, and me was to visit the local Anglican church and tour the adjoining graveyard. As she and I, at 8 and 7 years old, wandered the moors around our home in a rather remote area of northern England, we often stopped there.

The tenth-century Norman church, where Christians had sought solace and guidance for more than 1,000 years, stood beside the gently flowing river Dove, beloved by poet William Wordsworth and located just a mile and a half from our home.

One afternoon as Mary and I wandered hand in hand through the churchyard, past the graves where so many of our ancestors lay sleeping, we came upon a corner where there was a grouping of "newer" graves, with dates on the headstones about 1918 to 1919. As we knelt and deciphered the names and dates on the stones, we noticed that many of the dates of death were very close together, and, even more remarkably, the last names were often the same.

Mary, always of an inquiring mind, declared, "Boo [her name for me], let's go and find the verger [custodian] and ask him about it."

When we found him, he graciously accompanied us to engage in further inspection of the collection of graves and pointed out that they were family groupings. Then we all sat cross-legged on the grass, and he revealed to us the solution to the "mystery."

He told us that just after the end of World War I in 1918, a terrible epidemic, known as the Spanish flu, swept through Europe and England, killing many thousands of people. Because this was a previously unknown strain of the flu virus, no one had developed immunity to it. "People died like flies," he told us. Whole families, almost within days of one another, died as the deadly disease was passed from one to another.

"Come," he said, and he led us to a grave with a larger plot beside the banks of the river. He pointed at the names and dates—of birth and death—on the headstone. The last names were all the same. The dates of death were very close to each other, only days or weeks separating them.

"This family," he told us, "was almost wiped out within a very short time by the deadly plague."

Only one family member survived—the youngest daughter. She survived because she was not at home. She was just beginning her life's work as a servant to a wealthier family in another part of the country and, at the age of 13, escaped infection.

The brokenhearted girl, alone in the world, continued to work her way up on the domestic staff of several families and saved her hard-earned money, determined to have a tombstone erected in memory of her beloved family.

After a good many years she had accumulated enough money to make this possible. She had a stonemason erect a suitable headstone and had him engrave on it the names, ages, and dates of death of all the members of her family, together with a suitable quotation or Bible verse that she had selected for each one.

The last name to be added was that of their father, who was the last family member to succumb to the deadly disease.

Beneath his name she had the stonemason carve the words: "Our father was a loving man."

It was not until many years later, when I was grown and had children of my own, that I decided, privately, that if a tombstone were ever to be erected in my memory, I would want that same thing to be said of me by those who sought to preserve my memory.

Later still, as I contemplated that at-once tragic yet glorious "Easter" weekend when our Savior lay in the borrowed tomb for not quite three full days while all heaven was silent, I thought what a perfect "epitaph" that would have been had He "rated" a tomb of His own.

"I and my Father are one," He assured us (John 10:30). And to Philip He said: "Anyone who has seen me has seen the Father" (John 14:9, NLT).

In a way that—for now—we cannot fully understand, this was the Father, our Creator, God Himself, in the person of His Son, the Messiah, sleeping in the borrowed tomb.

How apt a memorial inscription it would have been: "Our Father was a loving man."

Indeed, He was, wholly and completely, a man, having laid aside His divinity and made Himself of no reputation, found in fashion as a man, made in the likeness of man. He experienced every aspect of human frailty so that we would see Him as He is, realizing, as far as is humanly possible, His limitless, wholly selfless love for us, His children, created by Him in His image, after His likeness (see Philippians 2:5-8).

The borrowed tomb did not remain sealed. Heaven did not continue to be silent.

Our Savior, our Father, emerged from the tomb, and the angels sang because, wonder of the ages, spectacle to the universe, "our Father was a loving man."

Chapter 2

"Comfort Me With Apples"

When I think of Aunt Bertha, long gone now, I see her so clearly, just as she looked so many years ago, a woman of indeterminate age, a tall, spare figure with graying black hair, wearing the inevitable long, black apron that she always wore, at least whenever I saw her.

Aunt Bertha was not actually my aunt. She was the younger sister of my beloved nanny, who "adopted" and cared for me from the moment I drew my first breath.

According to the prevailing custom, unfailingly Nanny was granted a half day each week to be free of the "day and night" care she was required to provide for me. Nanny's notion of an "afternoon off" was to take me to visit her unmarried sister, Aunt Bertha, in the little cottage she shared with her older brother, Harry, a tall, very quiet man whom I seldom saw.

Aunt Bertha, a "village beauty" in her youth, had been "crossed in love." A strikingly attractive young girl of 18, she had been engaged to be married to a local young farmer. Her future seemed assured. Three weeks before the projected wedding date, however, the groom jilted her and proceeded to woo and win a somewhat older woman, not overly handsome but heir to a considerable acreage of good arable and pasture land.

Bertha Fearn then announced her intention of never leaving the house again. And she never did. She spent a lot of time in her garden, a mix of fruit bushes and fragrant and beautiful with a profusion of flowers.

Aunt Bertha's specialty, though, was apples. Behind the cottage was a large apple orchard. Many varieties of apples flourished there, and Aunt Bertha tended them diligently and skillfully.

She also loved cats, many of which had free range throughout the premises and the outbuildings.

Aunt Bertha, who revered and adored her older sister, extended that adoration and acceptance to me. I adored her right back. I would follow her around (I was quite young) and "help" her in her garden. She was endlessly patient with me.

Mostly, Aunt Bertha kept her feelings to herself. I, though, was considerably less inhibited.

I recall seeing Aunt Bertha cry on only one occasion, at the time to me, as a very young boy, inexplicably. We were "working" in the flower garden. She had picked a bunch of the loveliest purple pansies to take into the house and was holding them close to her face to inhale the fragrance. She looked at them wonderingly, a faint smile on her often seemingly expressionless face.

I looked at her and got a glimpse, I later realized, of the lovely young girl she used to be.

"Aunt Bertha," I said, "you are so very beautiful."

"Oh, Boo," she said, half hiding her face in the blossoms.

Wonderingly I saw that she had tears in her eyes. Somehow I knew not to say anything.

Invariably, though, Aunt Bertha was firmly in control of her emotions, or appeared to be. "Come, Boo," she would invite, especially if she sensed that I was unhappy or upset about something. (I was an emotional child. Tears came readily to me.)

She would take me by the hand and lead me up the winding, wooden stairway to the apple loft, where the harvested apples were all spread out on old newspapers on the floor, sorted carefully into their various categories: Baldwins, northern greenings, russets, and various others.

We would sit companionably on a spread newspaper on the floor, savoring the exciting mingled odors of dust and mice. She would select a couple of apples for us from a pile of small red-and-white apples she referred to as "love apples," and we would sit there together, chewing our apples and enjoying each other's company.

We mostly said little. There was no need. I knew she loved me. She knew I loved her. It was strangely comforting.

"He brought me to the banqueting house, and his banner over me was love. . . . Comfort me with apples: for I am sick of [unwell because of] love" (Song of Solomon 2:4, 5).

Chapter 3

Prelude to
"The Beasts and the Children"

It was a bright, frosty morning when she came into my life totally unexpectedly. In her characteristically subtle and endearing fashion, she was destined to enrich it immeasurably.

It was the sort of day considered by most of the local gentry to be a great day for fox hunting.

My father, however, an ardent environmentalist and, in many ways, ahead of his time, was adamantly opposed to all of the "blood sports" much in favor by the "upper crust" of English society then and, to an extent, today. He denied access to his estate to any and all hunters, with or without titles and/or fortunes.

Foxes, being intelligent animals and long conditioned to struggling for survival, readily scented a safe haven from a considerable distance. During many a hunt, therefore, a frantic fox, hotly pursued by brave warriors on horses, accompanied by yelping, bloodthirsty foxhounds, would cross the boundaries of my childhood home and promptly "go to ground," attempting to find an adequate hiding place.

The hunt, with the hounds in full cry, would be brought up abruptly as my father fired his shotgun in the air and defied horses, men, or dogs to cross his boundaries.

My father was not, in any way, a violent man. On the contrary, he was notably compassionate, especially regarding those he termed, not without affection, dumb beasts.

He rarely raised his voice, and I saw him strike someone on only one occasion. In the course of one of his inspection tours of the home farm, he came upon a cowman belaboring a cow with a hefty stick. Panicked, the unfortunate animal was slow in making her way to where the man needed her to be.

"Stop," my father shouted. "Bend over," he ordered the startled farmhand. "Take hold of the hayrack and hold on."

Taking the stick from the now very unhappy man, my father proceeded to beat him briskly with it. Throwing the stick in a corner, he informed the man, now rosy-cheeked in all senses of the term: "If I ever learn you maltreated a beast again, you're out of here within the hour."

Then he proceeded to chat calmly with the man concerning farm matters. As far as my father was concerned, the matter was closed. He had taken care of it.

Not unnaturally, my father's views regarding fox hunting were not popular with the local aristocracy, who regarded him as a traitor to his class, which left him quite unimpressed.

"Call off the hounds," he ordered the master of foxhounds. "If one of your murdering hounds crosses my boundary, I shall shoot him dead."

By this time Nanny and I had rushed out to investigate the excitement. Nanny was brandishing her white apron at the bewildered hounds, which were now milling around the feet of the master of hounds, yelping wildly. He had them well trained, however. Lashing at them with his whip, he yelled at them to lie down, which, after a moment or two, they reluctantly did.

"That's the spirit, Nanny," called my father, who was evidently enjoying the neighbors' discomfiture. "You tell them. If a hound crosses over into our place, hit him on the head with that umbrella of yours."

Disappointed and resentful, the master turned his horse, the horn was blown, signaling "gone to ground," and the hunt began to move off.

"Look, look, Nanny," I squealed. "There's another little fox. See, the hounds are trying to catch him."

A streak of dark-colored fur emerged from what looked, from a distance, like the center of the pack of hounds, raced toward the greenhouses, and disappeared.

"I don't believe it was a fox, Boo," said Nanny, adjusting her apron and assuming a less belligerent stance. "I think it was a little cat. Let's see if we can find it. Poor wee thing. It must be terrified, and likely it was hurt, too."

It was a long, frustrating search, but neither of us was willing to give up. The thought of the poor, terrified creature dying in agony kept us searching.

Eventually, by sheer luck, I spied a movement at the end of a partially hollow log. Cautiously going closer, we identified the tip of a skinny tail barely poking out of the end of the log. The cat—for that indeed was what it was—had panicked, taken refuge in the log, and having come to a dead end, evidently lacked the courage, or was too cautious, to try to back out of its less-than-satisfactory haven.

"Run to the stables, Boo," Nanny instructed me. "Bring back one of the stable boys and a big pair of thick leather riding gloves. I'll stay and watch the log."

I was back soon with the stable boy, who, protected by the heavy gloves, pulled the little cat out of the log and held it out for inspection. The animal, inevitably still terrified, was a small female tabby cat with large, unusually expressive green eyes and a long skinny tail. Her only visible injuries were a tattered-looking ear, which had evidently been chewed briefly during her escape from the hounds, and what looked to be bites on the aforementioned tail.

"Take her to the stables, Henry," Nanny instructed the stable boy. "Put her in a box, harness up the pony trap, and take her to the veterinarian down in Sudbury. You may tell Higgins [the groom] I told you to go. You know where the vet is, don't you?"

"Yes, ma'am," responded Henry, taking a firmer grasp on his reluctant passenger. "I'll be off, then."

"Just a minute, Henry," I told the stable boy. "I want to have a look at her."

The cat and I observed each other, and, I believe, we both liked what we saw. In fact, she attempted a brief, tentative purr. At least I maintained she did. Nanny interpreted it as more of a growl.

"Her name is Peggy," I announced, skipping on one foot in my excitement. "She's my cat."

"We'll see," cautioned Nanny. "Mrs. Wilson [the housekeeper] is not going to like it. You know she hates cats."

"Pooh sticks!" I responded. (I was currently being read to from *The House at Pooh Corner.*) "She hates everything."

"Now, Boo," admonished Nanny, frowning, "watch your manners."

We didn't see Peggy for a week after that. When we were reunited, she was a good deal more prepossessing. She was clean. Her coat was shiny, and apart from her tail being a bit bent and one ear looking a little ragged, she seemed to be in good condition. I thought she was beautiful.

"Look, Nanny," I exulted. "She's as good as new."

In the subsequent weeks Peggy settled in as a permanent—indeed, privileged—member of our ménage. Nanny, who was a saint, and a determined one at that, "fixed" things with Mrs. Wilson, and Peggy became my devoted companion. She slept, albeit illegally, at the foot of my bed and followed me around like a dog.

Sometimes we would sit and look into each other's eyes and try to guess what the other was thinking. I believe she was better at it than I was.

Chapter 4

The Beasts and the Children

Although members of my family were not regular church attenders, we, by heredity and custom, considered ourselves members of the Church of England.

Not being part of a "religious" family, my sister and I were not exposed to, subjected to, or privileged to (your choice) take part in Sunday school, and attended Sunday services at the parish church only on special occasions.

It would be difficult for me to choose my favorite among the many days of special celebration in the church calendar, but I can readily arrive at a short list of four such annually recurring occasions.

Upon consideration, even though the Christmas Eve watch night service, when the manger scene "came alive" in celebration of our Lord's birth, was a strong contender, closely followed by Palm Sunday, when the girls and boys, in white dresses (the girls) and dark suits (the boys) strewed palm fronds (willow branches) along the path through the churchyard all the way to the church door, and Easter

Day, when the choir, accompanied by the organ and the unusually large congregation, sang joyously of our Savior's resurrection, none of these had quite the appeal for me that a lesser celebration did.

My slightly older sister, Mary, and I both eagerly anticipated the celebration of St. Francis Day. I was never quite sure whether we were recalling the day of the good saint's birth or remembering the anniversary of his death, but, in any event, this celebration was unlike any other throughout the Christian year.

Francis of Assisi being the patron saint of animals, our old and gentle vicar, the Reverend Roger Lejeune (he must have had Norman ancestry), took the opportunity to honor the long-deceased "brother" of the weaker ones" in a unique manner.

Special preparations for the celebration, known as the blessing of the animals, were necessary because of the unusual nature of the congregation and the celebrants. The stone-flagged floor of our tenth-century Norman church was piled thickly with straw all the way from the lych-gate entrance to the churchyard. Bowls of cold water were placed at strategic intervals in case any of the celebrants was overcome by an irresistible thirst.

Each member of the congregation, which was composed almost entirely of children, carried or led the creature selected to receive the priest's blessing.

When the verger (elder) gave the signal for the ceremony to begin, the long line of children, accompanied by those the good saint would have designated their "little brothers and sisters," began their slow progress up the straw-strewn nave toward the high altar, where the priest waited, his arms outstretched in welcome.

"Welcome to God's house, children," he said. "Welcome, little brothers and sisters."

My sister and I, toward the end of the long, straggling line, waited until it was time for us to move. This particular year my sister carried her current favorite pet, a hedgehog named (somewhat unimaginatively, I thought) "Prickles," which she had painstakingly and patiently "tamed" after having lured it to her by dint of numerous saucers of milk put out overnight for its delectation.

She had done a good job, and the timid little creature had become so accustomed to her that he (we thought) would uncurl from his prickly ball position and allow her to gently stroke his surprisingly soft and furry tummy. He would look at us with his bright little eyes and—Mary and I convinced ourselves—would "smile" at us as he poked his inquisitive little nose into our palms in search of the anticipated treat. Mary and I loved him dearly and were convinced he felt the same way about us.

In my arms I cradled Peggy, my cat. Peggy was not only my cat— she was my friend, confidant, and constant companion. Although less-discerning folks had described her as "scrawny," "puny," and "poor-looking," in my eyes she was beautiful, elegant, and everything a cat should be. For her part, Peggy, like most cats, recognized her true superiority and, from my sheltering arms, surveyed the motley assembly regally. Clearly Peggy was debating with herself whether, perhaps, she should bless the priest.

As each "candidate" approached the priest and presented his or her companion, he or she would reply, as seemed appropriate, to the reverend's query: "Boy or girl?" The child would respond: "Boy" or "Girl" or "I don't know, Father."

Father Lejeune would smile, place his hand gently and briefly upon whatever part of the proffered creature's anatomy was available to him. He would say "Bless you, brother hedgehog" or "Bless you, sister pig" as appropriate, and proceed to the next celebrant.

An emotional child, I always found the sight of our priest laying his hands on the beautiful, wonderful creatures I dearly loved intensely moving. And when I heard his gentle voice invoking a blessing on our humble "little sisters and brothers," I was inevitably, try as I might to control my "weakness," moved to tears.

Waiting in line with Mary, as the procession made its unhurried way along the nave of the church, I began to sniffle.

"I won't cry, Mary," I assured my sister, not very convincingly.

"Yes, you will," responded my sister matter-of-factly. "You always do."

My "big" sister, not unsympathetic but made of sterner stuff than I, knew me better than I knew myself.

Peggy, who knew me very well too, looked at me hard with her big green eyes, licked the tears from my face, and purred softly into my ear.

Chapter 5

The Night the Holy Spirit
Called on Me

A s a very young child, although officially and by heredity a baptized (christened) member of the Church of England, I had little contact with the church, as such, and no exposure to the Bible at all.

Nevertheless, by the infinite grace of my heavenly Father, I was, quite early, aware of the existence of the Holy Spirit, despite not having had a formal introduction to Him.

Growing up in a relatively remote, rural area of Derbyshire in England, in a house at the edge of the moors, I was essentially a solitary child. I spent much of my time roaming the moors, sometimes accompanied by my sister (my only sibling), but often alone, my only companion the sheep cropping the short, wiry grass that grew between the outcroppings of limestone rock.

Some would have said that the moorland was a wild, desolate place. To me, however, lying on my back in the heather and clover, it was the most beautiful place on earth. I lay there listening to the birds, the ripple of the trout stream, and the occasional bleating of the sheep in the distance, and if I had been acquainted with the concept, I would have thought that I was in "Eden."

I soon discovered, however, that as well as the sheep, there were other denizens of the moors, although not readily visible, all around me.

I discovered, as I lay there, half sleeping, half waking, that I was, indeed, not alone. I realized, to my astonishment and delight, that if I lay very still, made no sudden movements, and remained very quiet, other inhabitants of the moorland, curious about this strange, large creature, would conclude that I posed no threat to them, and very cautiously approach me. I knew they were watching me, alert for any movement, but fascinated by this almost daily visitor to their world.

Eventually, after a very long wait, and almost exhausted by hours of immobility and of trying to render myself invisible, one or the other of the "wild" moorland dwellers would, overcome by curiosity, summon sufficient courage to come close to me, sometimes even close enough to sniff at me, and, on occasion, astonishingly be bold enough to investigate at close quarters.

On these occasions, when the mouse, the bunny, even the lizard, crept, hopped, or crawled right up to me as I lay in the heather, even at times employing a part of my person as a vantage point from which to survey the surrounding landscape, my happiness was complete. I was in ecstasy.

Realizing that, to an extent I had not thought possible, the bunny, the mouse, or the lizard trusted me, I told myself that this beautiful, innocent, wonderful creature knew that I loved it and loved me back.

With eyes filled with tears, I asked myself, "Where did all this beauty, this wonderful world in which I find myself, come from? How—and why—did it come about? Who, what, made it, and for what purpose?"

Lacking a formal religious education, I was directed to the divine Teacher, the Holy Spirit, who impressed on my young mind that the

One who—I had heard my nanny say—created the world had made it. He had created it for me—because He loved me and wanted me to be happy.

Later, as I was exposed to smatterings of Bible stories, I began to identify the various members of the Godhead and become vaguely familiar with their names.

I had heard Nanny, who was an Anglican Christian woman, speak of Jesus' baptism and of the Holy Spirit, so far my anonymous moorland friend, coming to the Lord looking like a dove, a beautiful white bird.

As the year progressed and the balmy summer and autumn days gave way to winter, my days on the moor were suspended for a while.

I was never afraid of the dark. In fact, I found it comforting and somehow safe. Unless the wind was blowing the snow in my direction, I slept with my window partially open so that my cat, Peggy, could jump from the limb of the big tree outside my window onto my bed.

This was "illegal," but Nanny—dear, understanding Nanny—pretended that she was unaware of this.

One night following a particularly violent blizzard, after the snow had stopped falling and the wind had died down, Peggy and I heard a sound outside and went to the window to investigate.

Peering out into the darkness (what light there was reflected off the snow, which lay thick everywhere), I saw, clinging to the branch of "my" tree, the most beautiful and certainly the biggest bird I had ever seen.

It was pure white. It had big, round, yellow eyes, which were fixed on me as it swiveled its head from the side and clung to the branch of "my" tree with its fearsome-looking claws. It was making soft, murmuring sounds as it watched me.

I had never seen a more beautiful, astonishing creature in my life.

"Nanny, Nanny," I called excitedly. "Come quick! Come and look."

Nanny, who slept "with one eye open," rushed in from her bedroom nearby, pulling on her robe. "What is it, Boo?" she exclaimed. "Are you all right?"

"Oh, Nanny, look," I urged her, pulling her toward the window where the bird still clung to the limb of the tree, clearly unafraid of us behind the glass partition.

"What is it, Nanny?" I demanded. "Isn't it beautiful? Isn't it huge?"

"Yes, Boo," agreed Nanny. "It is indeed."

"Oh, Nanny," I pressed her, "do you think—do you think it's the Holy Spirit?"

Nanny, who always knew what to say, put her arm around my shoulders as we continued to watch the big, beautiful bird.

"No, Boo," said Nanny gently. "I don't think it is the Holy Spirit. It's a snowy owl, on its way from the Arctic, near the North Pole. I expect it got blown off its course in the storm and stopped here to rest before going on."

"Why did he stay right here, Nanny?" I asked her. "Did he know I live here? I still think it might be the Holy Spirit."

"You know what I think?" said Nanny. "I think Jesus sent this beautiful bird to call on you to tell you He loves you."

"Oh, Nanny," I cried out, "I hope he stays a while. He's so beautiful. I'd take care of him."

Nanny held me for a few more minutes. She often did that.

"I love you, Boo," she told me. She was crying.

In the morning, when Peggy and I woke up, the bird was gone.

I didn't say any more about it to Nanny—not just then. But it will always remain one of my fondest childhood memories.

"I will not leave you comfortless: I will come to you" (John 14:18).

Chapter 6

Pictures at an Exhibition

I spent very little time with either of my parents, and the infrequent periods I spent with my father were, therefore, something of a highlight in my experience.

On one occasion I was, in the seclusion of the nursery, asking Nanny questions about my family, about who my grandparents and great-grandparents were, and how we came to live as we did.

Nanny told me what she could and then said, "Boo, you should ask your father these questions. He would be better able to tell you what you want to know."

When they were not away, I saw my parents daily for a brief time. Each afternoon at precisely 3:30 my sister and I, freshly washed and dressed, with hair carefully combed, would be escorted to our parents' quarters for what I came to look on as the "interview." My mother would kiss me gravely on the cheek, and my father would pat me on the head and ask me if I was being a good boy.

Usually my sister, being more outgoing than I, carried whatever conversation there was. I fostered an ambivalent approach to these encounters. I suppose I unknowingly set myself up for inevitable disappointment. Having foolishly fantasized about a warm and tender exchange of affection, I really knew that the "visit" would, in reality, be impersonal and quite formal. As the clock struck 4:00 we, at least I, welcomed, with some relief, the arrival of the nursemaid to escort me back to the love and security of the nursery and reunion with Nanny.

Nevertheless, a few days after my conversation with Nanny, I summoned sufficient courage to address my father on what had been on my mind.

"Father," I said, somewhat diffidently, "I know my grandfather's name was John, and my grandmother's name was Mary. What were they like? What was Grandfather's father's name?"

My father looked at me, almost startled, for a moment, and then he smiled. Rising from his chair, he took my hand. "Come," he said.

Wondering, I followed him obediently.

Father led me through several corridors and another room or two until we stopped at the entrance to a long, narrow room that widened toward the middle, a bit like a pregnant corridor. The walls of this room were lined with oil paintings, framed in all sizes of frames, some of dark, old-looking wood, others in ornate gilded scrollwork.

"Now," said my father, "these are your ancestors. These are pictures of your grandparents, their parents, their parents, and so on."

I looked at the pictures in some amazement. My father led me down the rows of pictures and began to tell me who each one was and how he or she was related to me.

I don't recall exactly how old I was at this time. I must have been quite young, because my father hoisted me onto his shoulders so that I could see the upper of the two rows of pictures. I held on to my father's shoulder and felt at the same time deliciously excited and almost a little fearful. This was the first time I had ever experienced close physical contact with my father, and while the experience thrilled me, I felt strangely close to tears.

The whole experience made a deep and lasting impression on me. Young as I was, I sensed from my father's words that in some mysterious way I was linked to these distinctly odd-looking people dressed in—to me—very weird costumes. They were, of course, appropriately dressed for the varying periods in which they had lived, some of them even in suits of armor.

I suppose our half hour was miraculously extended on this afternoon, for we were in the gallery for quite a long time, as my father stopped by each picture and spoke briefly about the person portrayed.

I came away in a turmoil of very mixed emotions.

"There you are, then," said my father as we turned to leave. "That is your family; that is where you—and I—came from."

I don't think he expected any reaction—and he got none. There was too much to think about. He had, however, planted the germ of an idea that was to stay with me, for better or worse, for the rest of my life. In some mysterious way I was inextricably involved with these strange people, posing, in their outlandish clothing, for the portrait artist. I owed them something. Because of who they were—and who I was—I had to behave in a certain way. Because of them, there were things I could not do—and things I must do.

Back in the nursery Nanny told me, "I missed you. Did you see the pictures?"

"Yes, Nanny," I replied. "I saw the pictures. There were some very strange people, dressed in very funny clothes."

There was a lot more to it than that. I knew it. Nanny knew it too. But being the intuitive, understanding person she was, she did not press me. She knew that I needed time to digest what I had seen. Then, when I was ready, I would tell her—as best I could—what had happened to me.

Chapter 7

Floods of Tears and Small Potatoes

Maybe it was because Mary and I had happened to cross paths with little Sophie Giles that morning during our tour of two or three of the neighboring farms. Then again, maybe that chance encounter had nothing to do with it at all.

It was October—that glorious time in the moorland country of northern England. The heather was in full bloom, the gorse bushes were a blaze of gold, and the Canada geese were arriving daily in heart-stopping V's high in the windy sky to find nesting places for the winter on the relatively mild Gulf Stream-warmed shores of the British Isles.

It was also potato-lifting time, which enhanced the delights of these glories of the remnants of Indian summer. Many farmers, including Farmer Giles, Sophie's father, were busy in their potato fields digging the potatoes, preparatory to storing them in the straw and earth-covered clamps, or mounds, before the really hard frosts sealed the earth for the winter.

The attraction for Mary and me, though, was the inevitable bonfire in a corner of the field, over which hung a huge cauldron of boiling salted water. This is where the potato pickers (it was done by hand in those days) brought the pails of "pig potatoes," the very small potatoes, too small to be commercially useful, to be boiled for pigs and for any children who happened by. To Mary and me the tiny potatoes, fresh out of the bubbling cauldron, were food fit for the gods.

Joined frequently by the farm children, we waited impatiently for the tiny, delicious potatoes to be fished out of the boiling water. Blowing on them to cool them, we devoured them greedily, to the farm workers' amusement.

On the Giles farm the farmer's wife and younger children joined him and the other pickers in the field for the potato harvest, and Sophie, who was 4 years old, was also "helping," staying near to her mother, who kept a close watch on her youngest.

Mary and I had learned to understand the little girl's speech, not an easy task, because the child had a birth defect, which, I learned by questioning Nanny, was known as "cleft palate." This disability not only produced some deformity of her mouth and jaw, but hindered her from speaking clearly. Nevertheless, she seemed to be a happy, friendly child and was evidently thought much of by her parents and siblings, who joined us by the pig cauldron when it was time for a pause from the backbreaking task of gathering the potatoes.

Sophie's mother fished out some potatoes from the steaming cauldron for her youngest, blew on them to cool them, picked her up, gave her a loud smacking kiss, and set her down on a dry gunnysack to enjoy her treat.

Having eaten all we could hold and probably more than was good for us, Mary and I waved goodbye to the harvesters and made our way home to be cleaned up, dressed in more formal clothing than the print dress and shorts we wore, respectively, and prepared for our daily brief visit to our parents' quarters at 3:30 in the afternoon.

I was still thinking about little Sophie and her mother's evident affection for her when my sister and I entered the drawing room.

Our parents kissed us perfunctorily and inquired, as always, about our welfare. Mary engaged in desultory conversation regarding our activities, while I, more reticent, hovered in the background.

Finally it was time to take leave of our parents and return to our respective nurseries. The inevitable and acceptable procedure was for one of us, invariably Mary, to say, "Well, we'll see you tomorrow. Thank you for inviting us," and depart decorously.

This particular day, however, I, suddenly possessed by who knows what hysterical emotion, instead of behaving in the regular approved manner, rushed over to my mother and attempted to plant a passionate kiss on her cheek.

Predictably, my unfortunate mother, taken completely by surprise, recoiled in horror and firmly, not to say forcibly, pushed me away from her with a gasp of disbelief. The ceremonial "kissing" had already been endured. This uninhibited behavior was totally unacceptable.

Unreasonably, perhaps, I was totally devastated by my mother's reaction to my extraordinary behavior. I burst into uncontrollable sobs and ran from the room, closely followed by Mary, who, invariably in control of the situation, closed the door behind her and took me in her arms.

Chronologically not much older than I, but emotionally far more mature, she held me for a while and said nothing, while I buried my face in her soft brown hair and soaked the lace collar of her green velvet dress with my tears.

Finally I began to calm down some, and Mary, with perception way beyond her years, told me, quietly and firmly, "Stop crying, Boo. She really loves us, you know. She just doesn't know how to say it."

I didn't believe a word of it, but, calmed by my sister's embrace and her quiet voice, I finally got some sort of hold of myself and permitted her to lead me in the direction of my nursery.

Mary produced a lace-trimmed handkerchief from the secret

pocket all little girls had stitched onto their underwear in those days, and I dried my eyes and stopped shuddering.

"I'm sorry, Mary," I said, somewhat shamefacedly. "I'm an idiot. And I made you all wet. What will Nanny Hunt say?"

"Who cares?" responded my sibling. "And you're not an idiot. I'll tell Nanny Hunt there was a cloudburst in the drawing room. Come on, I'll walk you back to Nanny Fearn. They'll be sending out a search party if we don't get a move on."

We entered my nursery hand in hand. I didn't know what to say. Nanny, characteristically, waited for enlightenment.

Mary spoke for both of us: "Sorry we're late, Nanny," she apologized. "Boo didn't feel well in the drawing room, so I walked him back."

She turned to me. "Got to go," she said. She gave me a quick hug. "I love you, Boo," she whispered in my ear, and was gone.

"I was getting worried about you, Boo," said Nanny, ignoring my red eyes and disheveled appearance. "Tea's ready. Come on and sit down."

It was several days before I summoned enough courage to join Mary in the obligatory daily visits to the drawing room. Nanny made up excuses for me until she felt I had had sufficient time to rebuild my emotional resources in order to resume the ritual.

"I think you should go the drawing room today, Boo," she told me after several days had gone by. "You owe it to your sister."

As always, she was right.

Chapter 8

A Mother's Day Episode

Mother's Day was on the calendar for the immediate future, or "Mothering Sunday," as it was commonly known in England at that time.

Not yet commercialized, the recognition of the contribution of mothers was very largely a religious celebration, a relatively low-key event in the ecclesiastical calendar. Yet for some inexplicable reason, I felt, at 5 or 6 years old, that this year I must, in some way, demonstrate some sort of recognition of the day.

There were, of course, complications: For one thing, I was not at all close to my mother in any way. We lived our lives quite separately, though under the same roof, and my contacts with her were brief and quite formal. I had little reason to believe that she was emotionally involved with me at all.

I was cared for from birth by a loving, caring nanny, and my world involved only four with whom I had intimate contact: Nanny; her unmarried sister, whom I called "Aunt Bertha," and whom I, accompanied by Nanny, visited almost weekly; Mary, my slightly older sister; and Peggy, my cat.

I gave the matter some thought and devised a plan of sorts. I would approach the situation very delicately and restrain my emotions—not an easy or natural reaction for me.

I convinced my tutor, who conducted classes with me daily (which neither of us took too seriously), to take me into the village in search of appropriate greeting cards for the occasion.

After an exhaustive search we ended up at the little literature outlet that was a part of the church office and found a very limited selection of cards related to the celebration of "Mothering Sunday."

I selected three and headed home. I gave some thought to what I should write on each one.

Keeping as tight a rein on my emotions as I was able, I settled on as brief and "unemotional" expression of my feelings as I could manage.

I inscribed Nanny's card with: "To Nanny. I love you so much."

Aunt Bertha's read: "I love you, Aunt Bertha. Thank you for loving me."

The third one—intended for my mother—I left blank for the moment.

I was not disappointed by the reaction to my tiny offerings.

Nanny put her arms around me and held me for a long moment. I cried—of course—when she told me, "I'll always love you, Boo."

Next time we visited Aunt Bertha, I gave her my card.

Aunt Bertha, with tears running down her dear face, took me in her arms. "Oh, Boo," she said, and we cried all over each other.

Nanny and I went home, and I tried to pluck up my courage to send someone over to deliver my mother's card.

Despite a lot of heart-searching, I lacked the courage to write any of the things I desperately wanted her to know and wrote on my mother's card: "Happy Mothering Sunday—Amott." (She never called me "Boo.")

What little courage I had ebbed away completely. Sadly, I tore my card into tiny pieces and dropped it into my wastepaper basket. Then I cried a little, got undressed, and crawled into bed, soon to be joined (illegally) by Peggy, my cat, who observed me thoughtfully, licked the tears from my face, and went to sleep in my arms.

Almost uncannily, Nanny always knew what was going on with me. I believe she could read my thoughts.

The following morning she said nothing about the previous day.

"Boo," she said, "it's going to be a beautiful day. I'll ask Cook to pack us a picnic, and I'll send a note over to Mary to tell her to get ready and come on over from her nursery, and we'll go and have a picnic on the moors. There'll be gorse in bloom by now, and maybe some lambs."

"I will not leave you comfortless: I will come to you" (John 14:18).

At that young age I was, as yet, unfamiliar with this assurance given to us by our Lord. Throughout many years since, however, it has been a sure anchor to me through all kinds of vicissitudes and uncertainties.

Chapter 9

The Girl With the Emerald Eyes

The girl stood there, silent and still, holding her cardboard tray of short lengths of colored yarn.

The small boy, passing by with his ayah, tugged at the ayah's hand, bringing the two of them to a halt, and looked at the girl. His eyes—he did not know why—filled with tears.

It was hot—approaching midday on the Indian street. Bombay, for much of the year, is very hot and stiflingly humid.

The street was, as always, crowded—teeming with people, rickshaws, and some motorized traffic—and enveloped in a confusion of sounds, some relatively familiar, some exotic and to his unaccustomed ears strange beyond belief.

But for the moment the small boy, accustomed as he was to life in a remote English hamlet, to quietness and almost universal tranquillity, was oblivious to the cacophony of sounds and aware only of the young girl, standing alone on the sidewalk, surrounded, it seemed, by an aura of quiet—even, paradoxically, of solitude.

The child—perhaps about 7 or 8 years old, though it was hard to determine because she was so thin and fragile-appearing—was, as was customary at that time and in that place, quite innocent of clothing, a factor that added to the impression of vulnerability that defined her, a quality that, though he was not aware of it and was as yet unacquainted with the term (being only 7 years old), had, more than anything else, caused him to stop and had brought tears to his eyes.

He wept readily—too readily, some said—and if asked, he would have, employing what vocabulary was at his command, tried to explain: "She looked so defenseless—as if she might so easily be hurt. And she was quite beautiful."

It was perhaps her eyes that particularly drew his attention. Unusually, although her skin was a light brown and her hair, long and straight, hung, shining, to her slender waist, she had beautiful green eyes that held, to the perceptive onlooker, more than a hint of sadness. If pressed, the young boy would have said, "I think she often cries." And the thought of her crying made him cry too.

The other thought that came to his mind as he observed her was the notion—realization, perhaps—that "she has no idea how beautiful she is." She had no money for even the cheapest, simplest sari or garment of any kind, but she had tried, nevertheless, to "make herself beautiful" and more attractive by a colored glass bangle on each of her thin wrists (they were available for a tiny price in the bazaar) and another on one of her slender ankles. To complete the effect, she had knotted a piece of colored yarn into her glossy dark hair. Again, the young boy did not know why this moved him so and brought more tears to his eyes.

"Come, young sahib," the ayah urged, tugging at his hand. "Let us go to the hotel, where it is cool and where there are civilized people to look at."

"Ayah," said the boy, "you have my money in your purse. Buy the things she has. Buy all of them. And give her more than they cost—for *baksheesh* [tip money]."

"Young sahib," remonstrated the ayah, clearly becoming impatient, "you are indeed the strangest child I have ever had to care for. What use do you have for laces and pieces of yarn? They are worthless. Later we will return to the bazaar and find something of worth for you to take home."

The young boy continued to look at the girl, who remained standing, seemingly oblivious, in the inadequate shade of a building, silent and, it seemed, eternally patient.

Although he could not have put his intense feelings into words, he knew, nevertheless, that he longed to take care of her somehow. She looked so alone.

He stood his ground. "Ayah," he said, so loudly that it surprised even himself, "do as I say. Buy all that she has—and don't forget the *baksheesh*. I wish it. Then, perhaps, she can go home."

Grumbling, the Anglo-Indian nursemaid did as she was told. She grudgingly opened her purse and, closely watched by the young boy, gave the girl money. The boy, inclining his head in a gesture of respect, accepted the tray of trivia from the girl.

The young girl, delighted, looked at the boy, smiled sweetly, placed her thin, brown hands together in the universal gesture of gratitude, turned, and was gone.

"Now," said the ayah, in some exasperation, "perhaps we can return to reality and go back to civilization."

The young boy did not hear her.

Chapter 10

"It's Going to Be All Right"

Many years ago when Mary, my sister, and I were quite small, we would play in the trout streams that crisscrossed the moorland near our home in the north of England.

England no longer has any working coal mines, but back then there were many, and quite a few in the area where we lived.

Mine accidents were relatively frequent, and if the wind was in the right direction, as we played we would sometimes hear the siren from the pithead of a mine, alerting the mining families that there was trouble underground.

The women and children, alerted by the siren, would drop everything and rush over to the mine and wait anxiously at the pithead, praying for the safety of their beloved husbands, brothers, lovers, and others who were trapped in the darkness, often a mile or more below their feet.

Hearing the sirens, Mary and I would scramble out of the water, shake ourselves like two puppies, and kneel down on the grass and heather; then Mary, as the older, would pray that Jesus would take care of the children's daddies who were down in the mine and that somehow it would be "all right."

I cannot help relating these experiences to the time, a good many years later, when I went to "say goodbye" to my precious little son, about to lose his battle with leukemia.

Adrian (Ady), although not quite 4 years old, was quite convinced that it was going to be "all right"—that Jesus would "make him all better."

As time went on, though, and it began to seem clear that, short of a sudden miracle, this was not about to happen, even Ady, whose faith was much stronger than that of many of those much older than he was, began to wonder how much longer he must wait for Jesus to answer his prayer.

I tried to explain to my little boy that even if for reasons unknown Jesus did not "make him all better" right away—even if he too died, as he was well aware that many of his fellow sufferers had before him—certainly when Jesus came to wake him up and I came to meet him, he would indeed be "all better," just as Jesus had promised.

This was a difficult concept for a tiny boy. Perhaps even more difficult for a daddy who had prayed with him.

I tried hard to believe. I held his tiny hand in mine. He looked so small and vulnerable.

"Is it going to be all right, Daddy?" he implored, squeezing my fingers as tightly as he was able. "Oh, Daddy, is it going to be all right?"

"Yes, darling," I assured my little boy. "Yes, Ady, it's going to be all right."

His little fingers relaxed their grip.

A single tear escaped and trickled down his cheek.

He essayed a faint smile, closed his eyes, and went to sleep.

He believed me. He believed that amazing truth that was difficult for me to grasp and to hold on to.

He believed that this would be so, because "Daddy said so."

"Except you become as a little child," our Savior told us, "you will not be ready to enter the kingdom of heaven" (see Matthew 18:3).

"I cannot explain it all to you now, my son," the Lord told Job (see Job 38–41). "You would not be able to understand. But remember this: I love you. Trust Me."

We are children of a common Father. Trust Him. He loves you. Believe—because "Daddy said so."

Chapter 11

The Enchanted Princess

And whatever did the prince do then?" inquired Wendy excitedly. "How did he get through the maze?"

"Well," I replied, slowly and clearly, raising my voice above the "crump" of another high-explosive bomb and the slow thunder of falling masonry, "he suddenly remembered that he had the magic necklace in his pocket, so he took it out and began to count the pearls again . . ."

My voice trailed off as I pushed my "tin hat" up off my forehead and wiped away the sweat with my free hand. I wondered how much longer it would be. I reckoned that the odds were about fifty-fifty that the other fellows would tunnel through before the rest of the house collapsed. I couldn't see my watch in the pitch blackness, but I supposed I must have been in here two hours already, and "Jerry" was still pretty busy around the dock area by the sound of things. Yes, it was 8:00 when the siren went, quite a bit later than usual. I closed my eyes. I could hear it now—my landlady's voice . . .

"Arthur, Arthur, wake up. Jerry's over. I thought we were going to have a quiet night for once. Get your trousers on. Here's your tin hat and your gas mask. Got your flashlight? Cheerio, then, luv; just be careful. I'm just going to make Dad and me a nice cup of tea. Sounds like Commercial Road's catching it again. Wonder if our aunt Ethel's all right."

"Cheerio," I called as I dashed for my bicycle. "Tell Jimmy I'll bring him a nice bit of shrapnel."

I was 17 years old—almost 18—so I had dropped out of my college freshman year anticipating inevitable "call-up" (drafting) for service very shortly. World War II was already under way, and I opted to spend my "waiting period" working with the Air Raid Precautions people in London. The "Blitz" was already devastating large sections of Britain's cities, especially the East End of London—the dock area.

I was billeted with a family in that neighborhood and was assigned to a Heavy Rescue Squad in a heavily bombed area not far from the docks.

The Heavy Rescue Squad sent me and three others to an "incident" that had been reported at the north end of Commercial Road, just behind Millwall Docks, one of London's most important—and heavily bombed—commercial areas. Two pairs of duplex houses had received a direct hit from a high-explosive bomb, with the possibility of survivors buried in the debris.

It took the truck a half hour to get there, although it was only a couple of miles normally. They were redirected through a couple of detours because of bomb craters and an unexploded land mine in the Caledonian Road. When we arrived, the wardens had already dug out three bodies—two women and a little girl—but they had not been able to move the heavy timbers and masonry without equipment.

The sky over east London glowed red from the burning docks. I glanced around me momentarily. It was the old familiar pattern: waves of bombers with incendiaries, followed by second and third waves unloading high-explosive bombs inside the ring of flame.

As I watched, a barrage balloon went up in a spurt of flame like a rocket, and I could see the flash and hear the bark of the antiaircraft guns on Hampstead Heath. A fighter plane streaked across the sky, belching a burst of tracer, and the acrid, suffocating stench of the smoke screen stung my nostrils.

I was brought back to reality and the task in hand by a shout from the crew captain. Joe Burns was a big, red-faced man in his early 40s. He was a stevedore by trade, and I had heard tell that Burns could carry 300 pounds on his back. I was inclined to believe it.

"Come on, Arthur, lad," bawled Joe. "What you're looking for— Goering? He ain't comin' tonight. Called me and said as he couldn't make it. As 'e 'ad a date with Frow Gobbles."

I shook myself, pulled my crowbar and hatchet from my belt, and turned toward the wrecked houses. The local warden was briefing the Heavy Rescue crew.

"This 'ere 'eap of bricks and glass," he was saying, "is numbers 6, 8, 10, an' 12 Commercial Road. As far as we know, there were seven people in the four 'ouses when they was 'it. We're got out three—all goners. So there's probably some others somewhere in that lot—nippers too. We moved what we could with our 'ands, but didn't durst shift it around too much . . ." He broke off at a hail from the other warden.

"'Ere, George, give us a 'and with this 'un. Alive, I think."

The two wardens heaved up on a heavy beam that lay across what had been number 4, and Joe got his big shoulders underneath it, groped around a bit, and came out carrying a woman. She was streaked and smeared with blood and grime, and her left foot dangled uselessly from a broken ankle. She was crying.

"Take it easy now, missus," soothed big Joe, cradling the woman in his arms as if she were a baby. "You'll be as right as rain in a minute."

The woman quieted down momentarily, and then she sat up, glared around her wildly, and began to cry afresh.

"Wendy," she sobbed. "Where's my Wendy? She's still under there. Put me back in there. I'm going to get her . . ." Her voice rose to a scream.

"Now, now, missus," remonstrated big Joe, stroking her hand and talking to her as if she were an infant. "It ain't a bit o' use you carryin' on like that. Pull yourself together, and give us a bit of information. How old's Wendy? What room was she in? Was she in bed? Just whereabouts was she? Anybody else in there?"

From the woman's somewhat incoherent story the facts were pieced together. Dad was at work down the docks, and Wendy, who was 10 years old, and her mother were in bed in adjoining rooms when the bomb fell. That was it—the rest we would have to find out for ourselves.

"The trouble with this 'ere job," said big Joe, hunching his broad shoulders, "is that the 'ole ain't very big, an' if we start to shift the debris about much, the lot'll come down and she'll be crushed as flat as a kipper—that is, if she ain't already . . ." He paused and glanced around him at the crew.

"Reckon as I'm the smallest," I said. "Give me the kit, Joe."

It took me a half hour to find her. I didn't dare move more than an inch or two at a time, pushing the debris ahead of me with my hands and putting props behind myself with the bits of wood that I stumbled across. The third time I stopped and listened, I heard her. She was crying quietly.

"Hey, there!" I called. "Wendy, where are you?"

The cry stopped abruptly, and a small voice, which sounded almost beside me, answered. "I'm here," said the voice. "Who are you, and why do you talk so funny? I thought you were never coming. Where's Mum?"

"Half a minute," I responded, smiling to myself in the darkness.

"One at a time. My name's Arthur, and I'm talkin' funny because my nose and throat's full of dust. Doesn't your mum ever sweep your bedroom floor?"

The child laughed—a high, uncertain sort of laugh.

"Where's Mum?" she insisted. "Is she dead? Have you got her out yet?"

"Mum's all right," I reassured her. "She's out. Hurt her foot a mite, but nothing to shout about."

"Honest?" persisted the child. "Or are you stuffing me?"

"Cross my heart," I swore. "I never tell lies to a lady."

It took me 10 more minutes to get to where she was. She was lying flat on her back, and a heavy beam lay across the lower part of her legs, pinning her down. I could see at once by the light of my flashlight that I could do nothing alone.

Upon inquiry, I elicited the information that she wasn't hurt, but that her legs and feet felt dead and that she was thirsty.

"Righto," said Joe at the other end of the "walkie-talkie" telephone line, "we'll start tunnelin' right away. You don't think as it'll hold up too long, eh? Well, we'll be as quick as we can, but we'll 'ave to shore up as we come, y'know. I shouldn't give her no morphia unless she really needs it. I've told her ma as you've found her."

"I liked that one," said the child. "Coo, you don't 'alf know a lot of stories. My dad only knows about three, and he tells me the same ones over and over. Wish he was 'ere, though—no, I don't," she said softly.

"Well, go on," the child persisted. "What's the matter? Have you gone to sleep?"

I cleared my throat and tightened my grip on her hand.

"Well," I continued, "he took the magic necklace out of his

pocket and began to count the beads, and like I said, the thirteenth one was the one." I paused for breath and inspiration and continued.

"He rubbed this one in his hand, and just like a flash of lightning, the maze and all the horrid creatures disappeared, just as if—as if a bomb had hit it."

"Go on, go on," urged the child, clapping her hands and laughing delightedly. "It's just like us, isn't it? You're the prince, and I'm the beautiful princess with the ringlets."

"Yes," I agreed a little gruffly, "it's just like us."

London's dockland smoked under the early-morning sun. Big Joe, sitting at the desk in the Heavy Rescue Squad headquarters, chewed his pencil and looked worried. He picked up the incident report sheet and read what he'd written so far.

"Y'know, Arthur," he confided, heaving a deep sigh, "next to fetchin' out dead 'uns, I 'ate this part of it the worst. I can't never think what to put. What did them nurses say about 'er?"

"They wouldn't say anything definite," I replied. "She's all right herself. They didn't know about her feet, though. Nice kid. She seemed more than 10, somehow."

Big Joe Burns signed again, took up his pencil, and resumed his writing.

"An incident was reported at the north end of Commercial Road at 8:00 p.m.," he wrote. "The house was demolished, and it was found that a girl was under the debris. The above-mentioned then proceeded with caution . . ."

He looked up and grinned as the siren sounded a long, steady note—the "all clear."

Chapter 12

The Runaways

It seems strange that out of all the hundreds—maybe thousands—of faces, young and old, that I saw during those nightmarish few days, I can recall only one. Really recall, that is. The rest of them waver in and out of my consciousness—vague phantoms of a time I would just as soon forget.

This one face, however, refuses to be dismissed. It belonged to a small boy. I do not know his name. I do not know where he came from or where he was going. I cannot forget him.

"All you got to do, mate," I was assured by a passing British soldier—like me, a member of the British Expeditionary Force in France in late May 1940—"is follow your nose. Just keep headin' toward the smoke and the 'ellish racket, and you'll get to Dunkirk and, if you're lucky, back to England, 'ome, and beauty."

So I kept on walking, with air becoming smokier and the explosions getting louder and more frequent with every mile I covered.

I had plenty of company. Troops of my own and a number of other armies passed me continually, most traveling in the same direction I was headed, and a few, inexplicably, heading in the opposite direction.

The general impression was one of total confusion, although surprisingly there was little panic. The British and French soldiers with whom I shared the road seemed to pay scant attention to what was going on around them. Like me, they were close to exhaustion, and with a weird singleness of purpose they doggedly trudged on toward the coast and the pall of smoke in the distance. Some still carried a field pack, while others had discarded everything except their rifles for easier traveling. Occasionally I would see a soldier with a dog straddled across his pack or perhaps a small child riding piggyback on his shoulders.

The traffic was not all military, however. There appeared to be at least as many civilian refugees on the road as there were retreating soldiers. At times the roads were jammed with old men, women, and children, encumbered by all manner of loads and bundles, fleeing from who knows where before the advancing German army. Some of them pushed rickety handcarts piled high with a few pitiable remnants of their homes. Some trundled ancient baby carriages with two, three, or more infant passengers. The elite among the refugees pedaled vintage bicycles.

As the miles unrolled, the wheeled traffic became less frequent as the exhausted travelers, one by one, abandoned their possessions by the roadside. Their treasures had become mere impediments that hindered them in their race for survival. The weary mothers, big sisters, and grandfathers hoisted the littlest ones onto their backs, grasped the hands of those who were old enough to walk, and struggled on. They were, by this time, dirty, disheveled, tired out, hungry, and terrified.

The troops and the civilian refugees paid little attention to each other. Their only real contact came when soldiers and civilians alike made a dive for the same ditch as the Luftwaffe planes screamed down to strafe the straggling figures on the crowded roadway.

It was immediately following one of these increasingly frequent retreats to the hedgerows that I encountered him. Scrambling back onto the roadway, I perfunctorily brushed the twigs and leaves off my clothing and sat down at the edge of the road to empty the water out of my boots. The two of them—the small boy and the middle-aged man—scrambled out beside me and, like me, paused for a moment's reorientation before resuming their flight.

The man walked with a pronounced limp, which doubtless explained why he was not in uniform. He was unmistakably French. The boy, about 6 years old, was, equally unmistakably, his son.

Neither of them spoke to me, nor did they say anything to each other. The man looked at his son and made a halfhearted attempt to brush off the child's ragged clothing. His boots caused him no problem, as he wasn't wearing any. The boy looked at his father.

After many years, the expression on the face of that young French child continues to haunt me. It has borne with it emotions of anger, of frustration, of guilt that this was the kind of world we had bequeathed to our children.

The boy's big, dark eyes, fixed earnestly on the man, reflected no fear. The expression in the child's eyes was one, rather, of total bewilderment. His world had suddenly become incomprehensible. For the first time in his short life he had come face to face with something that was too big for his father to handle. He was not so much afraid as totally uncomprehending.

The sound of the planes died away in the distance. He stood up and trudged on.

Almost immediately, however, the eyes of the travelers turned apprehensively to the skies again as the ominous sound of aircraft engines returned. This time a concerted attack by fighters and fighter bombers screamed down on the straggling refugees. Most had no time to dive for the sheltering ditches. They began to run—wildly, purposelessly, without direction. I ran too.

I continued to run for a very long time. I ran for several years. I too ran wildly, purposelessly, and without direction in an attempt to escape the God who had permitted such a hell on earth, who had done nothing, I felt, to protect the innocent.

No less bewildered than the little French refugee boy, I too thought that I was face to face with something too big for my Father to handle.

I continued to run. One day I ran right into the arms of my Father, who, amazingly, was running to meet me. He held me close, and I stopped running.

"This is my son," He said. "He was lost, and is found."

Chapter 13

Auf Wiedersehen

Nothing in six years of war, of death and desolation, had prepared me for the incredible horror of the Nazi death camp at Bergen-Belsen.

Belsen—the name of one of the most notorious of Hitler's death factories—has since become almost a synonym for horror, but incredibly, the impact of degradation and inhuman cruelty practiced by human beings upon other human beings has faded somewhat. But then, seeing for the first time what had previously been only rumored was devastating.

As the British troops entered the camp, few of the surviving inmates had either the strength or the will to register any reaction. Even then, after the German burial details had been working around the clock to destroy as much as possible of the evidence of what Belsen had been before the Allied forces arrived, it seemed there were more dead than living souls in the vast area of the camp.

I had been assigned to work with an information-collecting detail to gather data, partly for the use of the International Red Cross in their monumental—and almost hopeless—task of reuniting survivors, and partly for the use of what was subsequently to become the War Crimes Commission.

While most of the troops were deployed in organizing conscripted ex-guards and German civilians to bury the dead and care for the sick who remained barely alive, I took my sheaf of papers and sought out the Lagerführer.

Many eyes followed me as I made my way through the camp, some hostile, some pleading, the majority seemingly expressionless.

Pausing momentarily to jot down names and addresses of relatives provided me by those who were able to furnish information in the forlorn hope of being reunited with their families if they survived, I eventually located the Lagerführer. He had shut himself in his office in an effort to escape the fury of the liberating troops and the additional hazards of the typhus-ridden camp. I introduced myself. He told me his name was Ernst Oberheuser. This is his story.

He began with a sort of apologia for himself, for his camp, for the Schutzstaffel—the SS—to which, he told me, he had the honor to belong.

"You look at me as though I were less than human," he accused me. "You know nothing. You are young. You have seen nothing. You are unmarried, yes?"

I nodded assent.

"Let me tell you, Englander," he continued, "if you were a married man with a family, and you knew that unless you obeyed your orders—no matter what they entailed—you and your family would very soon find yourselves in the same situation as those poor wretches you are so busy burying outside, what would you do then, Englander?"

He didn't seem to expect a reply. It was a question I didn't want to answer.

"It took strong men to run the camps," he went on. "We SS

found it a very difficult and often unpleasant assignment."

I told him that I could well imagine this to be true.

"Some were not so strong," he continued, "and they did not survive. Let me tell you of my friend—my best friend and comrade—Klaus. He was a good man, but he was not sufficiently strong."

Oberstleutnant Klaus Schuler—Oberhauser's friend—was also a Lagerführer, but at Auschwitz, the vast death camp not far from the city of Munich.

Schuler had worked his way up to Lagerführer in Birkenau—a reception camp for Auschwitz—and was thoroughly accustomed to close association with all kinds of suffering, agony, and death.

As part of his duties, he would frequently meet the "transports"—the sealed cattle-car trains that ceaselessly rolled into the camp railway siding with their human cargo.

The sight of the dead and the dying, the young and the old, being off-loaded from the fetid cattle cars in which they had been sealed many days, had become commonplace to him.

One September evening, however, suddenly it was different—or it seemed so.

This particular transport included a large number of children. In the "selection" process that determined which transports would live until they died of exhaustion, disease, or suicide and which would go straight to the gas chamber, the youngest ones—those below 10 years of age—being too young to be useful as labor, soon, by the logic of the times, found themselves separated from their relatives, stripped of their clothing, and standing naked and shivering outside the "bathhouses"—in reality, of course, the extermination chambers.

Schuler was overseeing the herding of the latest crowd of unfortunates into the bathhouses when something unprecedented caught his eye. He noted that one little Jewish girl—she looked to be about 7 years old, just about as old as his own little Ilse—had somehow contrived to retain possession of her teddy bear.

When the condemned ones were stripped of their clothing,

everything else was supposed to be taken from them by the *kapos*. They were to leave the world as naked and free of material encumbrances as when they entered it.

But this little one, by some quirk of inattention on the part of the kapos—although she, like all the rest, had not a stitch of clothing—had kept hold of her toy bear.

Schuler's first reaction was to snarl to one of the kapos to take the toy from her, but something about the child—something he couldn't identify—prevented him from giving the order. Perhaps it was because she was more attractive than most of those who arrived at the gas chamber. She had not been in camp long enough to become a living skeleton like those who enjoyed a few weeks' reprieve from liquidation, and her face and body still retained the appealing softness and vulnerability of innocent childhood.

This factor, and the fact that she reminded Schuler of his own small daughter—except that his Ilse was blond and blue-eyed (a true Aryan), while this little one had olive skin, long black hair, and lustrous dark eyes, which she fastened on him—held him back.

Thrusting aside the screaming, lamenting ones who crowded around, he approached her.

The child shrank back but did not cry out, only clutched her little white bear more tightly. He tapped her gently on her shoulder with the butt of his pistol. "Child," he asked, addressing her in Yiddish, "what is your name?"

The child looked up at him. Tears had made twin tracks down her cheeks, but she met his gaze unflinchingly.

"I am called Esther, Herr officer," she told him in her high, clear voice.

Schuler stooped and tapped her on the shoulder with his pistol for the second time. "You may keep your bear, Esther," he told her.

He turned on his heel and walked away. He didn't want to see the packing of the gas chamber with the condemned ones. It was always the same anyway. The first few entered quietly, believing they were indeed going to bathe, as they had been told. Quickly disillusioned, some tried to scream warnings to those still outside, but to no avail. Driven by the clubs, whips, and rifle butts of the *kapos,* it was a brief task to herd the entire group into the chamber until the room was packed to the doors.

The smaller children were frequently flung on top of the mass of writhing, screaming bodies so as to take advantage of all available space before the doors were shut and sealed.

Then the trapdoor at the top of the chamber was opened, the cyanide pellets were introduced, and the trapdoor was closed.

Schuler knew from long experience that it took five or six minutes—or a little longer—for all the occupants of the chamber to die—agonizingly and painfully. He waited until 10 minutes had elapsed and returned—he could not have said why—to the chamber.

The *kapos* had opened the doors, the bluish haze had dissipated, and they were throwing out the bodies like so much cordwood for transportation to the crematoria.

By the wildest chance, Schuler saw her—her little body distorted in agony, her big, dark eyes dilated in horror—flung on top of a pile of bodies just beside the door. This time he could not meet her eyes, although they could no longer see him.

Oberstleutnant Schuler entered the now almost empty chamber, faintly nauseated by the lingering odor of the lethal gas, and walked toward a small, white object that had been kicked into a corner.

The Lagerfuhrer stooped, picked up the small, white teddy bear from the cement floor, tucked it under his arm, and strode off to his quarters. He felt he needed a drink.

For more than an hour Schuler sat at his desk in his locked office, though he was well aware that he had pressing duties elsewhere in the camp. His Mauser revolver lay on the desk in front of him. The toy bear sat on the desk to his left. Close to his right hand he had placed a bottle of vodka and a glass.

Schuler alternately cursed and prayed—for he had been reared a Christian—and drank. He felt as if he were going mad. Even the good Russian vodka failed to still the turmoil in his soul.

By this time it was quite late. The noises of the camp had subsided, and except for an occasional scream from the prisoners' huts, he heard nothing except the beating of his own heart. No one came by. No one sought him for any reason.

Klaus Schuler took another draught from the glass of vodka in front of him and banged his fist on the desk in an agony of frustration and self-condemnation. There was no one to offer a reaction of any kind. Only the bear sat there, unblinking, seemingly staring at him accusingly with its black, shoe-button eyes.

Oberstleutnant Schuler cursed, swept the bottle and glass off the desk with his arm, picked up his revolver, and fired at the bear.

The bear toppled off the desk and fell to the floor, a neat hole drilled through its middle.

No one paid any attention to the shot. In this palce shots, screams, and violent death were 24-hour, everyday occurrences.

Five minutes later another shot rang out from the locked office, then silence.

"This was in Auschwitz, you understand," the Bergen–Belsen Lagerführer reminded me. "After my comrade shot himself, his things were collected and forwarded to his widow in Hohenbrunn. I think they even sent the bear. She was informed that he had died in action, and he was posthumously awarded the Iron Cross. Soon after, I was transferred to Bergen–Belsen.

"So you understand," he pressed me urgently, "it was not always easy for those of us who held positions of authority. You do understand?" he inquired anxiously. "We had no choice. We had to obey orders. I, myself, what could I do? I was just *eine kleine mann,* a little man."

He opened a drawer in his desk, took out a letter, and proffered it to me. The envelope was soiled and crumpled. It had evidently been around some time.

"He wrote a letter," he went on. "Before he . . . did what he did . . . my comrade wrote a letter. It is to his wife and daughter. I have kept it. He was my friend.

"Will you ever be in the neighborhood of Hohenbrunn?" he inquired earnestly. "Here, I give it to you. If you ever get to be near there, you must take it to her."

He did not explain why this responsibility, suddenly, had become mine. He did not seem to think an explanation was necessary.

Almost mesmerized by a situation that had become close to unreal, I took the letter and placed it in the inside pocket of my battle dress.

I completed my questioning of the Lagerführer and took my leave. I did not see him again. Two days before I left the camp, my duties completed, he was shot.

When I accepted the letter, I had no intention of attempting to deliver it, even if this were possible. Nevertheless, I found myself unable to forget it.

I tried to put it out of my mind—even contemplated throwing it away or destroying it—but I could do neither. It had become something of an obsession. From what kind of home, I asked myself, did such a man come? What kind of people were his wife and daughter? How much did they know of the wartime activities of their "heroic" husband and father?

I "organized" a 10-day leave and contrived, by utilizing any of the allied transport heading in that direction, to make my way to the small town to which the letter was addressed. I told the drivers from whom I cajoled rides that I was looking for a woman. This they could understand.

Berating myself for a fool, I succeeded, by employing my fractured German and showing the letter, to find the street indicated on the envelope. Like most German towns at that time, it was a conglomeration of destruction and standing buildings, although not as severely damaged as many I had passed through.

I whistled to a boy playing in the gutter and beckoned him over.

Showing him the letter, I asked him if he knew where the house was that was indicated on the envelope. He led me to understand that he did, but that the woman to whom the letter was addressed no longer lived there.

By employing my German and his English, which were about on a par, I gathered that he knew where she had moved to, and was willing to take me there if I made it worth his while.

Not for the first time I was thankful that, although a nonsmoker, I always collected my cigarette ration for use as currency. I bribed him with a packet of English "Woodbines," and he escorted me to a small, only slightly damaged house about three streets distant. He indicated the door, took his payment, and left me on the doorstep.

With mixed feelings I knocked on the door. My heart was beating rapidly, and my mouth felt dry. I saw the curtain twitch at the tiny window, and a moment later the door opened.

I was confronted by a pleasant-looking middle-aged woman with graying hair. Clinging to her skirt was a small blond-haired girl. The child had very blue eyes and looked to be about 8 years old.

The woman looked anxiously at me. She took in my uniform and—to my great relief—addressed me in a semblance of English.

"Yes?" she inquired. "What can I do—?"

"I have a message for you," I told her. "May I come in?"

She neither acquiesced nor refused, but opened the door wider and motioned me inside. She indicated a chair, and I sat down. She remained standing, facing me. The child stood and gazed at me, a finger in her mouth.

After assuring myself that she was indeed the woman I sought, I tried to tell her that I had by chance met a comrade of her late husband's and carried a letter for her that he had entrusted to me.

I handed the letter—still unopened—to her. She examined it closely, holding it gingerly, as if it were a bomb, but made no move to open it. The child evidently wasn't sure whether to be fearful or excited.

Then, apparently sensing that I wasn't about to apprehend or denounce her, the woman relaxed a little and invited me to have coffee.

I was well aware that nothing approaching real coffee had been available in Germany—except in certain circles—for years, but I was unprepared for the remarkable concoction I was served. It was, I believe, made from acorns and other odds and ends, and it took quite an effort to force it down.

The little girl stood and watched me solemnly. Taking a couple chocolate bars from my pocket, I gave them to her, and she smiled for the first time, her blue eyes shining.

Emboldened by my gesture of friendship, the mother beckoned and led me to the one other room of the house—evidently the sleeping quarters. She pointed out a picture on the wall above the bed. It was a photograph of a middle-aged man in an SS uniform. He had assumed a stern pose for the occasion, but his face looked kind.

"My husband," she said. She had tears in her eyes.

I nodded. I turned to leave the room—and stopped. My last lingering doubts as to the real identity of the woman and her small daughter were dispelled.

On the opposite wall of the tiny room was a framed picture of a small blue-eyed girl with long blond braids—without a doubt the child in the next room, now sitting on the floor, her bare feet sticking out in front of her, slowly and ecstatically nibbling one of her chocolate bars.

The child in the photograph was wearing a short blue dress to the front of which was pinned a row of medal ribbons above an Iron Cross. She was clutching a small white teddy bear. The child had attempted to place her small thumb over a hole in the bear's middle, but a blackened ring of singed fur was plainly visible.

Suddenly I wanted to leave. I felt as if I were in the presence of the dead.

I turned and saw that the woman was watching me. Our eyes met, and we noted each other's tears without remark. I stumbled clumsily into the other room and proceeded to take my leave. The woman took my hands and thanked me. *"Danke schoen, mein herr,"* she said. *"Danke schoen."*

The woman still held the letter—unopened—in her hand.

I paused momentarily on the doorstep.

"Auf wiedersehen," said the woman.

"Auf wiedersehen," echoed the little girl.

I waved my hand. *"Auf wiedersehen,"* I called back.

I have no idea how much the widow knew of her husband's wartime activities. Maybe nothing—maybe everything. When I embarked on my journey to find her, I fully intended to tell her where I got the letter and what I knew of the circumstances of its writing. Maybe it was all in the letter, anyway. I don't know. I am certain that the little girl knew nothing of the true situation. The expression on her face as she stood there in her best dress, wearing her father's medals and holding the toy he had sent her, reflected the purest pride.

I thought about it all the way back to my base. Jolting along in trucks, in staff cars, in jeeps, even—miracle of miracles in those days—a short distance in a train, I struggled to decide whether I should have spoken, as I had intended.

But seeing the child seated on the floor, her bare feet crossed before her, her mouth smeared with chocolate, I lost my resolve.

All I could find it in my heart to say was *"Auf wiedersehen, Frau Schuler. Auf wiedersehen, kleine Ilse . . . Auf wiedersehen."*

Chapter 14

"May I Share Your Daddy?"

A drian was very sick. He didn't really feel too bad, but his mommy and daddy had to take him to England so he could go to The Hospital for Sick Children in London. The family had come from England to East Africa when Adrian had been a baby. Home to Adrian was the school compound near the big city of Nairobi, where the sun shone almost all the time except during the rainy season.

There were always many interesting things to do on the mission. Adrian's mommy and daddy were busy most of the time, but there was always someone ready to play with him. There was always someone willing to go with him to look for chameleons in the bushes at the back of the house or for weaver birds' nests in the jacaranda trees or the nandi flame trees that grew around the little school and church.

When the other children were in school, Nzorka, the Kikuyu garden boy, or old Isaac, the cook, would sit with him under the frangipani bushes to watch the termites or to tell him stories. Adrian didn't understand all the stories because they were told partly in

English and partly in Swahili, but that didn't matter. He just liked to listen. He liked to watch Nzorka and Isaac as they talked and as they smiled at him. He knew they loved him.

But now they were all gone—Nzorka, and Isaac, and Isaac's little boy, Chomba, and all the other children, too. He missed them very much. Really, they hadn't gone away, but he had had to go away from them.

When Adrian and his parents were leaving the mission, all their friends came to say goodbye. Some of them began to cry. Chomba had big tears running down his cheeks. Adrian almost started to cry too, except that it had been such a long time since anyone had paid so much attention to him and hardly any to baby sister.

He and Mommy and Daddy and baby sister got into Dr. Allen's car, and Dr. Allen drove them to the big airport in Nairobi. It was fun to get on the big plane and fly all the way to England.

But now that seemed a long, long time ago. Mommy and Daddy had taken him to the hospital, where all the doctors and nurses and even the maids were White people. They were very kind to Adrian. He liked the room they put him in. There were five other children in the room—three girls and two boys—nearly all the same age as Adrian. Although all the boys and girls were sick, they did have lots of fun together.

Adrian didn't mind the man who came in every day and took a little drop of his blood from his finger, but he didn't like the big needle they had to stick in him every day to give him the medicine he had to have. That really hurt, but, as Daddy said, it could be worse.

Every day Daddy came to see him. Daddy usually came every day just after lunch. He stayed all afternoon and ate supper with Adrian and even got him ready for bed. Then he would have a Bible story and prayer with Adrian before going home to Mommy and baby sister.

All the children in the ward played with Adrian's daddy. They even came around when Daddy told Adrian a Bible story and had prayer with him. There was one little boy in particular who liked to be around Adrian's daddy. That was Raymond. He seemed to think that Adrian's daddy was his own daddy, too. Whenever Daddy came to the hospital, Raymond would wobble across to him as fast as he could and hold up his arms to be picked up. Daddy would pick him up and carry him over to Adrian's bed.

At first Adrian didn't like it. Daddy had come to see him, not Raymond. It was his daddy. But Daddy explained to Adrian that Raymond was only 3 years old. He came from the Falkland Islands, which Daddy said were 10,000 miles away across the ocean. Raymond had been in the hospital so long that he had forgotten what his own daddy looked like.

Adrian thought about that for a long time. He wondered if he would be so brave if his daddy were so far away. Raymond fell down often, too, but he never cried. He had a disease that made his elbows and knees big and knobby. He couldn't walk every well.

So Adrian didn't really mind anymore that Raymond wanted to share his daddy. He knew that Jesus would want him to share with Raymond. And he and Daddy talked it all over. As Daddy said, Jesus had shared his Father with us, and God had shared His Son, Jesus, with us so that we could go to heaven when Jesus comes.

Adrian was glad that was settled. It made him feel so much better. He took a tight hold of Daddy's hand and smiled and went to sleep.

Chapter 15

Sheila's Wings

"I expect I shall have wings," Sheila confided as I sat on the edge of her bed. She and my young son were patients in the "terminal ward" of the Hospital for Sick Children in London, England.

"I expect I shall be able," Sheila continued, "to fly all around heaven, which is even more beautiful than Cornwall."

Cornwall, on England's west coast, was where she had spent her last—and final—vacation.

It is not usual for 10-year-old girls to dwell upon their inevitable and imminent demise, but Sheila was perfectly aware that, short of a miracle, her time on this earth was fast running out.

She was, however, not really looking toward the impending "event" with trepidation, or even devastating grief, but rather with anticipation. Sheila was not consumed with fear and uncertainty; she knew, courtesy of the sweet Holy Spirit, that everything was going to be better.

There was more. I held her hand, and we discussed it at length.

Guided, I truly believe, by the Holy Spirit, to whom I had prayed earnestly for direction, I did not embark on an attempt to delineate to my young friend my beliefs and my "understanding" concerning the state of the dead.

Sheila, properly and, yes, happily, was concerned, not with how it would be to "go to sleep," but how it would be when she woke up.

I was not about to debate with her concerning her belief that she would "fly" immediately from her grave into the arms of the waiting angels, who would take her to meet Jesus. The lapse of time, the "sleeping period," it seemed to me, was irrelevant, the "minutia" determined only by one's concept of time.

One's child falls asleep, and, as far as he is concerned, the next thing that happens is when he opens his eyes and hears his mother's voice: "Good morning, sweetheart. Time to get up."

Our Savior made no differentiation between what we call "sleep" and what we refer to as "death." I think of the precious young daughter of Jairus, the ruler of the synagogue. When the "mourners" saw Jesus, who had been called to the sick child's bedside, they were lamenting and wailing and tearing their clothing to demonstrate their "grief."

"You are too late," someone likely accused Him. "The child is dead."

Incredibly calm, Jesus ignored their ostentatious lamenting. "She is not dead," He asserted. "She is sleeping."

And they "laughed him to scorn" (Mark 5:40). He didn't know what He was saying. They had seen her.

Jesus dismissed the mourners and went with her parents into the room where she lay. He looked down on the little girl, Jairus' precious, lovely daughter.

His eyes, I suspect, were filled with tears—tears partly of sorrow for the lamenting, unbelieving ones, partly of joy because He was about to "wake her up," to repeat what He had previously done. He was about to give her life.

He looked at the child with infinite love and compassion. "Wake up, child," He told her. "It's time to get up."

The child stirred at the sound of that voice that alone can pierce the tomb, opened her eyes, and sat up.

She climbed off the bed and ran into the outstretched arms of her weeping, almost-unbelieving father.

"She will be hungry," Jesus reminded her parents. "Give her something to eat."

The "gospel," the story of salvation, that demonstration of our heavenly Father's unconditional, all-abiding love for His children, is not about the "state of the dead." It is entirely, always and always, about the gift of life that He has given to us and that, by sacrificing His own Son, He will give us again.

"For God so loved the world, that he gave his only begotten Son, that whosoever believeth in him should not perish, but have everlasting life" (John 3:16).

Our Father loves His only Son with a Father's yearning, all-embracing love. Yet, wonder of the ages—are you ready for this?—He loves you more.

He was willing to put the universe at risk, to risk eternal separation from His beloved Son, in order to give you—you—eternal life.

With David the shepherd boy, king, and forgiven sinner, I too must acknowledge: "Such knowledge is too wonderful for me, too great for me to understand!" (Psalm 139:6, NLT).

Chapter 16

Marilyn

E ven for a 3-year-old, Marilyn was tiny. Sitting up in her high-sided
crib in the "terminal ward" in the Hospital for Sick Children on
Great Ormond Street in London, England, often attached to sundry
tubes, wires, and other paraphernalia, she looked like a baby.

And quite often she sounded a lot like a baby, too, especially if
she was feeling particularly uncomfortable, and her mother, who had
to work to support her little family, was not currently with her tiny
daughter.

At such times little Marilyn would sit up in her bed and, with
tears, voice her lament to any who would listen.

"Mommy, Mommy," she would call, as loudly as her tiny voice
could manage, "he'p me, he'p me."

To Ady and I, listening to her plaintive appeals from across the
small ward, it was heartbreaking.

Like my not-quite-4-year-old son, Marilyn was a victim of a
form of childhood leukemia and was, therefore, a patient in the small

children's ward for leukemia and other child cancer patients.

Officially titled the "Mr. Punch" ward, with reference to the decor and the decals on the walls of the "Punch and Judy" puppets popular at the time, the ward was—not by reason of insensitivity but for practical reasons—often referred to as the "terminal ward."

None of the 10 or 12 child patients, whose ages ranged from infants to the "senior citizens" of 12 or 13 years of age, had, at that time (the 1960s), any reasonably optimistic expectations, but, mercifully perhaps, the very young were unaware of this.

The older children, of course, were well aware that to put it diplomatically, their prospects were not good. From time to time I would engage in a fruitless evaluation of which situation was worse, from the point of view of the parents and the children—the situation of the very young, "unaware" tinies, or that of the older "savvy" youngsters who "knew the score." Either way, it was nothing less than heartbreak. I suppose it was a case of "choose your heartbreak."

During the Sunday evening "support" meetings that the caring, compassionate ward sister (head nurse) had set up for parents and others to communally engage in prayer—if requested—and mutual encouragement, I was frequently faced with a question (more of a demand, really): "You contend that your God can heal our children. You say He loves them. Why does He refuse to heal my Marilyn, my Carolyn, my Jeremy? Doesn't He really care? Can He do it? Is He really there?"

Burning, viable questions, to be sure—questions with no easy answers. Questions that too often hit too close to home.

To return to Marilyn: Ady and I shared very compassionate feelings for Marilyn—or "the baby," as "big boy" Ady referred to her. Her plaintive cries of "He'p me, he'p me" always reduced us to tears.

From time to time, when she was not currently tethered to some apparatus for transfusion or infusion or other, the nurses would allow me to lift her from her crib and carry her over to Ady's bed, and we would sit and hold her and attempt to comfort her.

Frequently, after a time, a few hiccups, and a long sigh, she would calm down, nestle between us, and, on some infrequent but heavenly occasions, essay a smile.

Sometimes Ady would sing to her. She liked that and occasionally would even "sing" with him.

Inevitably, as I entered the ward one morning to spend time with my little son, I observed immediately that Marilyn's crib had gone, replaced by a new, freshly made up child's bed.

I said nothing; neither did Ady. Nobody made any comment. It was not that sort of ward. It was just something nobody could bear to talk about.

I don't know what was going through Ady's mind. A thoughtful child, he frequently "kept his own counsel." But I had an inkling.

My precious, compassionate little boy survived Marilyn by a couple months.

Then, on a glorious, sunny April day, we laid him to rest in a little country graveyard to await the sound of dear Jesus' voice: "Come, Ady; Daddy is waiting for you."

My little boy's faith never wavered—that "Jesus will make me all better."

Maybe that was the message the assembled parents were looking for at our hospital support meetings. They were, perhaps, appealing to the wrong person.

Chapter 17

"Thank You for Wanting Me"

S he was only 7 years old, tall for her age, with long, flaxen hair and big, green eyes. I missed her so very much.

My daughter Veronica, familiarly known to those near to her as Noni, had traveled from California, where we lived, to visit relatives in England. She had been gone six weeks. It had seemed to me like six years. Now—hallelujah!—she was due back in San Francisco the following day.

Noni and I adored each other. My unquestioning, unconditional love for this—to me—incomparably beautiful little person grew daily, along with her legs and arms. And now the day of her return was finally near.

I slept little that night. I arrived at the airport early, willing the airplane to land ahead of schedule.

The flight from London was announced as "arriving on time." The passengers filed out of the plane exit tunnel into the arms of waiting greeters. It seemed to take hours. Finally I spotted the person who was bringing Noni home. She was alone—no Noni.

The explanation provided was to the effect that, unbeknown to me, it had been decided to leave Noni in London "for the time being." She had been enrolled in a "very good" boarding school, and arrangements had been made for her to spend vacation time with her grandmother, a sweet, caring Jewish woman. "She is perfectly all right," I was told. "It will be good for her."

I was devastated. Clearly this was totally unacceptable!

Fast-forward three weeks, during which time I made arrangements for my precious little girl to fly home in the care of a female flight attendant.

The great day finally dawned. I waited, again, on the concourse for the arrival of the flight from London to be announced. I could not sit still or control the trembling of my hands. When, finally, the moment arrived, my emotions were barely under control.

I can never forget what I saw: My beautiful little daughter, tall for her age but terribly, unbearably vulnerable in her new school uniform, a little round beanie atop her long, golden hair, came toward me holding the hand of the flight attendant. I knew I had never in my life seen anyone more precious, more beautiful.

The flight attendant shook my hand, and I thanked her as best I could for caring for my daughter. "Noni is a sweet little girl," she told me, hugging my precious child before departing.

Noni and I fell into each other's arms, and our tears mingled and fell onto her shoes.

"Noni, oh, Noni, my darling," I said. "Were you afraid?"

"No, Daddy," she assured me. "I knew you'd come and get me, or have someone bring me home."

On the drive to our house in the Napa Valley, we kept touching each other to reassure ·ourselves that each of us was really there. Neither of us said very much—not then.

Partway home, though, Noni said, "Daddy . . ."

"Yes, darling?"

"Thank you for bringing me home. Thank you for loving me."

And later, just before we reached our home on the campus of Pacific Union College, she said, "Daddy . . ."

"What is it, sweetheart?"

"Thank you, Daddy. Thank you for wanting me."

My eyes filled with tears. I was unable to utter a word.

Now, these many years later, I have adopted my little daughter's words as my own. In each bedtime prayer, just before the final amen, I tell my Savior, my heavenly Father: "Thank You, Jesus, for coming to get me—for bringing me home. Thank You, Father, for loving me. Thank You, Father, for wanting me."

This love of my heavenly Father so far transcends even my love for my children that I cannot, in this life, encompass it. Like David before me, I cannot help exclaiming: "Such knowledge is too wonderful for me; . . . I cannot attain unto it" (Psalm 139:6).

And so I simply pray again and again, "Thank You, Father. Thank You for wanting me."

Chapter 18

The Kiss

Veronica, the elder of my two daughters—and most often referred to as "Noni"—was, right from the start, a notably determined girl. When Noni decided that something was going to happen, she would make it happen.

There was the incident of the baby bunny when she was about 7. At that time Noni was attending the local village school, and each day she walked to and from school—about one and a half miles from our home on the campus of Pacific Union College in California.

Noni's passions embraced many things, but "creatures"—including whatever walked, crawled, slithered, hopped, swam, or flew—were high on the list of her concerns.

One day on the journey to and from school, Noni noticed a tiny baby rabbit hopping in and out of a hollow tree by the roadside. Very excited, and with that determined glint in her green eyes that I knew so well, she told me, after she got home, "Daddy, I'm going to catch a baby bunny."

As usual, this was a statement, not a possibility. Noni's vocabulary did not include the word "maybe."

"Honey, I am not sure that is really a possibility," I replied. "Bunnies move very fast, you know. And they have very good hearing."

Noni fixed me with her steady gaze. "Daddy, I'm going to catch a baby bunny."

Privately I doubted the possibility of a successful culmination to the project, but I said no more.

A couple of weeks went by, and, I learned later, Noni passed by the hollow tree each day on her way home from school, knelt down near the opening, and waited.

Actually, a day short of two weeks later, with shining eyes and a small bulge evident under her blouse, she confronted me with—I should have known—the fait accompli. "Look, Daddy. Isn't he sweet? How old do you think he is?"

"Oh, sweetheart, he surely is a darling little fellow. But I don't know if you will be able to rear him. He is very young. I hope he doesn't die."

Again, I should have known.

"I can rear him, Daddy. He won't die. I love him. I won't let him die."

He didn't die. With the tender care of his new "mother," he grew and became very "tame" and accustomed to close association with humans.

There was, however, one drawback to the arrangement. We (Noni, mostly) tried very hard to help to integrate him into the family of "domestic" bunnies we already had. They lived in an erstwhile wine cellar near the big old house that was our home. The floor was covered deep in straw, and the furry denizens frolicked around freely within a considerable space.

Although he did try to join the group and become a member of the "family," Bunny, for whatever reason, was never accepted by the "domestic" group. Eventually he gave up trying and sat by himself in a corner of the cellar, ignored by the others, waiting for "mother" to get home from school to cuddle him, talk to him, and love him.

Rabbits grow and develop rapidly, and it wasn't long before Bunny was pretty well full-grown, a mature but, sadly, often lonely bunny.

This concerned me, and I knew that it seriously bothered my daughter, who loved him too. Finally I said, "Noni, dear, I don't think Bunny is really happy. I know that you take the greatest, most loving care of him, but he needs other bunnies, and our 'tame' bunnies won't accept him. I think, perhaps, it is time to take him back to his 'wild' family. I'm sorry, darling."

Noni, with Bunny in her arms, had tears in her eyes. She said nothing for a moment.

I had tears in my eyes too.

Then she looked straight at me, in the forthright manner I knew and loved. "You want to kiss me, Daddy, don't you," she said.

It wasn't a question.

I took my precious, determined, caring little daughter in my arms and kissed her. Our tears mingled and fell onto Bunny's soft fur as he nestled in her arms.

The next day, after school, we took Bunny back to his, we surmised, birthplace. I hung back and waited while Noni said goodbye to Bunny and released him at the entrance to the hole in the hollow tree.

He sniffed briefly and disappeared.

My daughter returned to where I waited. Again we held each other and wept together. Then we said a prayer for Bunny and went home.

That was many years ago. Noni is now the wife of a Seventh-day Adventist minister and the devoted mother of four young adults, two of whom are married. Yet I will never forget the day when, while holding a much-loved bunny in her arms, she told me, in effect, that she knew perfectly well that I loved her.

And I know perfectly well that God loves us. I have long believed that a "message" of every story, every parable, every incident recorded in His Word—the "love letter" He has left for us—is the same: "I love you."

It was in the fields not far from Bethlehem that the shepherds heard the angels singing joyously: "Glory to God in the highest, and on earth peace, good will toward men" (Luke 2:14).

The shepherds, their eyes turned toward the sky, followed the star toward Bethlehem seeking Him, "Emmanuel, God with us," a baby, lying in a manger, come to repair the broken relationship between our Father and His beloved children.

He loved us, so He told us so.

Chapter 19

A Reason for Being There

Some time ago I had occasion to pay several visits to a house in my community where I became acquainted with a young girl, about 6 years old, and a tentative friendship was formed between us, despite—or perhaps because of—the 50 years difference in our ages.

It was the sort of home that I was not accustomed to entering—but I had business there. My first impression was the general air of dishevelment and the strong odor of marijuana that permeated the atmosphere. Three children, including 6-year-old Jennifer, all rather sketchily clad, tumbled over one another on the unswept floor. The young parents, totally ignoring the children, were engaged in a spirited verbal battle, liberally laced with colorful epithets.

Not many weeks later this young couple, who, although both married, were not married to each other, decided to "split" and promptly left the area, taking the two smaller children with them, but—her parentage apparently being a matter of some discussion—abandoning the 6-year-old to her own devices.

Subsequently, a compassionate Christian couple in the locality took the child into their home, and she appeared one Sabbath morning in my second-grade Sabbath school room.

Jennifer was clean, attractively dressed, and, I quickly perceived, very frightened by the totally unfamiliar surroundings in which she found herself. The preliminary song service was already under way, so I smiled at her, found her a seat, and sat down beside her. A few minutes into the program a small hand timidly crept into mine, and a voice whispered in my ear, "I'm glad you're here."

Not infrequently I have been moved to ask myself: "What are you doing here? Are you serving any genuinely useful purpose?"

Now, as the tiny fingers tightened around mine and I looked into Jennifer's anxious little face, I realized that I was there, at that moment, in that place, specifically to be a bridge over troubled water for one very bewildered little girl.

As Christians—followers of the compassionate Jesus—we too often forget that we are here, in this place, at this time, for that very purpose: to reach out to those who are hurting and desperately need an expression of His love.

The needs to which James addresses himself in the biblical book named after him—for impartiality, a gentleness in communication, humility, a concern for economic justice, and a desire for heavenly wisdom—are all rooted in a concern for those around us.

Such a mutual concern for others, both within and without the church, establishes a path to unity, a sure and simple antidote to the current climate of divisiveness that sets brother against brother and renders ineffectual the presentation of a loving Savior to those who look for Him in us.

Chapter 20

Whoever

I truly believe that, by the infinite grace of my heavenly Father, my very earliest teacher and guide, in my barely formed searchings after a knowledge of my Creator and for the reason for my existence, was none other than the sweet Spirit.

As a very young child I was arduously and totally fascinated by the beauties and wonders of nature, by the natural beauty of the countryside where I was born and grew up, and the wonder of the myriad creatures that inhabited it. My home on the edge of the moors was to me the most beautiful and enchanting place in the world.

Growing up in that quiet, almost uninhabited environment so many years ago, I was permitted almost complete freedom. As a young boy I spent countless hours lying quite motionless in the heather, my only companions the sheep cropping the short, wiry grass that grew between the outcroppings of limestone rock that flanked the trout streams, which flowed, clear and cold, in and out of the caverns that were part of the moorland landscape.

It was so very quiet: no sound but the faint sound of the bleating of the sheep in the distance, or, once in a while, the tinkle of the bell around the neck of the old bellwether—the sound that helped the shepherd locate the flock as the animals wandered the trackless moorland in search of pasture.

I was so blessed, surrounded by the "sounds of silence."

I lay motionless in the heather, listening to the almost imperceptible sound of the tiny wild honeybees, or "mossy toddlers," as the country children called them, and the occasional cry of a bird. I knew that I was in "Eden," although I was, not having had exposure to the Bible, not yet familiar with the term.

I had learned from almost daily experience that if I lay quite still in the heather, made no sudden movements, and made no sound, the wild denizens of the area would, slowly, little by little, overcome by curiosity, lose their fear of me. They would realize that I meant them no harm, that I had no desire to hurt or capture them, and, I convinced myself, they would know that I loved them.

And when, after a prolonged wait, one or other of the "local inhabitants" would approach me, sometimes even employing some part of my anatomy as a temporary resting place or as a vantage point from which to survey the surrounding landscape, I would look at the bunny, the mouse, even the lizard through tear-filled eyes. I was in ecstasy. My cup of joy was full.

I wondered as I lay there who—or what—had made all the beauty, all this wonder, and why. How did it come about, and what did I have to do with it?

I, as yet, knew little or nothing of God, of Creation, of my place in the universe. I decided to call whoever, or whatever, was responsible for all that enchanted me "Whoever." Looking toward the heavens, I whispered, "Thank You."

Later, much later, as I was exposed to God's Word and learned who indeed had designed and created all this beauty and wonder, and, even more incredible, had made it and brought it into being for me, I was delighted to come across the account of Paul's experience when he saw the shrine "to the unknown God" in Athens and told the people "whom therefore ye ignorantly worship, him declare I unto you" (Acts 17:23).

Sometimes, in my musings, I fantasize that, when I get to heaven or to Eden restored, my Father, who, I know, has a sense of humor, may greet me: "Greetings, my son. I am 'Whoever.' Welcome home."

Chapter 21

"He Touched Me"

Advancing age and diminishing eyesight have taken their inevitable toll, so I no longer drive. I must rely on proffered rides to my church (20 miles distant) if I am to attend Sabbath service. Consequently, there are weeks in which it is not possible for me to meet with the other church members for worship.

However, as always, by the grace of God all is not lost.

On the Sabbaths when I am "homebound," I call my "congregation" together for our very exclusive, albeit unorthodox, worship service. Actually, a "call to worship" is not necessary. My fellow congregants—Amber, my 12-year-old pit bull/yellow Lab mix; Mr. B, my very large tabby-and-white tomcat; and Tabitha, my somewhat smaller black-and-white female cat—upon seeing me arranging our four seats in a row and collecting my Bible and songbook, eagerly and without prompting settle themselves in the "pews" and look at me in anticipation.

They, my boon companions, are a "model" congregation. They

are very attentive and wholly cooperative, and they "can't wait" for the proceedings to begin.

We start with prayer. I gently place their front paws together (we don't insist on closed eyes) and offer a brief petition to our common Father/Creator, inviting His presence in our humble little gathering.

Then we read (I read; they listen attentively) a verse or two from our Father's "love letter" addressed to each of us.

I remind Amber, Mr. B, and Tabitha that our Father knows their names, and as I mention their names, they murmur and purr as they hear their own name repeated.

Then we come to what, I believe from observation, is their favorite part of the "service." It is time to sing.

Our tastes are simple and direct. We favor short, lively gospel choruses, preferably with an appropriately lively "beat."

Then I ask for suggestions. Interpreting the evident "body language," I always am led to finish up with what I recognize as their favorite song. They always ask for "He Touched Me." It is an "action" song.

Each time we get to the phrase "He touched me," I place my hands gently and caressingly upon each of my congregants in turn. They love that part.

They've even got the "hang" of the melody and murmur and purr the "descant." I know the angels are singing with us.

We close with prayer, thanking Jesus for loving us and for giving us each other. Then we say amen, each in our own way, and reluctantly separate, not for long nor to go too far.

I sort of imagine that if Francis of Assisi, the patron saint of animals, was still with us, he would graciously accept our invitation to worship with us and maybe to address our little gathering. I believe that he too, at the appropriate point in our favorite song, would gently place his hand on each of my precious companions.

Our Father, who designed and created each one of us, is indeed a sensual God, in the original and essential meaning of that often misused term. He "speaks" to us—all of us—via the senses that He built into each of us, regardless of how many legs we have.

And we, by His grace, respond, each of us in our own way, and He understands. "For where two or three are gathered together in my name, there am I in the midst of them" (Matthew 18:20).

Chapter 22

In the Presence of Angels

A couple of blocks from my home in Kennett Square, Pennsylvania, the self-styled "Mushroom Capital of the World," is an apartment building, home to several Mexican families, the fathers being workers in the mushroom farms that surround the little town.

I walk by this apartment house almost daily and have made the acquaintance of several of the families living there, especially the many beautiful, delightful young children who have, delightfully, accepted—even "adopted"—me as one of their own.

They call me "Grandpa" (I am 84 years old), and they are a significant blessing (happiness) in my life. I live alone, except for my dog and my two cats, and always look forward to passing by this dwelling.

The children—of both sexes, assorted ages, and varying degrees of familiarity with the English language—flow out in a body when they are aware of my approach, and, all talking at once, tell me in a mixture of English and Spanish all about what is going on in their exciting young lives, confident that this is just as important and meaningful to me as it is to them. And it is.

One day I was returning from the post office with my mail, and just as I neared the house where my little friends lived I tripped on a broken part of the sidewalk and fell flat on my face, my mail scattering in all directions and my walking stick and my glasses flying off elsewhere.

Hearing the confusion, my young Latino friends rushed out in a body to investigate and found me lying prone on the sidewalk somewhat bruised and much disheveled.

Greatly disturbed by their dear "Grandpa's" predicament, they rushed to my aid, chattering away in Spanish and English.

"Oh, Grandpa, are you all right? What happened? Are you all right? Have you 'disturbed' your bones?" they inquired anxiously.

With a concerted effort they helped me to my feet, brushed me off, patting me solicitously, some of the tinier ones crying piteously in sympathy.

The "team," directed by one or two of the older girls, collected my scattered mail, found my glasses (miraculously unbroken), recovered my walking stick, and with many sympathetic queries as to my welfare, and some tears, pointed me in the direction of my home.

I made movements, stiffly, toward proceeding homeward.

But no . . . this would not do at all.

"No, no, Grandpa. We will take you home."

The decision was unanimous. My remonstrances fell on deaf ears. So I surrendered, I admit, gratefully.

"Oh, children, thank you so much. But you must tell 'Mamacita' where you are going so she knows where you are."

This done, we set off in a body, my guardian angels still chattering away excitedly, each one, small and larger, trying to get as close to "Grandpa" as possible so they could touch some part of him, with an eye to be ready to catch him if he should suddenly fall again. Our little procession proceeded slowly and cautiously the couple of blocks to my house. My "saviors" insisted on getting me safely inside my house before they headed for home. I thanked them, again and again, so very sincerely for their caring, gentle love and help. I told them that I loved them.

And the angels—the ones with wings—sang.

And I shed a few tears—not because of the pain from my bruises, but because of wonder and gratitude at my precious little friends' concern and love for me.

Later that evening I heard a gentle knock on my door.

Two of the older girls, each carrying a bowl covered by a clean white cloth, greeted me: "Grandpa, are you feeling better? Mamacita sent you some beans and some soup. She said to tell you she is praying for healing for your bruises."

The angels—I heard them—sang again.

Chapter 23

One Small Boy

Kobe, a little boy of my acquaintance, is one of the children with disabilities cared for lovingly and compassionately by a special friend of mine, now a nurse specializing in pediatric care, a woman whom I have known since she was 12 years old.

When visiting her, I have had the privilege of meeting Kobe, and I am kept aware of his progress and have grown to know him over several years.

Kobe, now of preschool age, was born with multiple "birth defects." Kobe, however, does not in any way consider himself disabled. This beautiful little boy is one of those spoken of by the poet William Wordsworth as coming from God "trailing clouds of glory."

I have never met a sunnier, more charming, courageous person of any age than this young child. He is, or appears to be, unaware of his "limitations." He strives valiantly to employ and develop the capabilities he has, and has made astonishing progress in the ability to walk, to communicate understandably, and to achieve a level of independence that is almost unbelievable.

One aspect of living that this little boy finds no difficulty in excelling in is the capacity to give and accept love. He is perhaps the most "loving" person I know.

In spite of his limitations, he is rarely, if ever, downcast. When, teasingly but not unkindly, he is asked by an adult, "How's my bad boy?" Kobe's response, in his "broken English," is "I am not a bad boy. I good boy. I happy."

And he is.

To know him is to love him. It just cannot be otherwise.

Blessed by a caring, loving family and a loving, compassionate caregiver, Kobe responds, expressed to the best of his ability: "I love you, Daddy. I love you, Mommy. I love you, Miss Jeannette" [his caregiver].

I know that when Jesus comes and Kobe will walk straight and tall and will speak clearly and coherently, his parents, along with many others whose lives this little "bruised lamb" has touched, including his own beloved Miss Jeannette, will rejoice, albeit with tears, but they will be tears of joy.

I know this will be so, for we have our Father's promise: "Weeping may endure for a night, but joy cometh in the morning" (Psalm 30:5).

"Even so, come, Lord Jesus" (Revelation 22:20).

Chapter 24

"All the World's a School"

With most profound respect to my compatriot William Shakespeare: he got it almost right! Your precious children, like mine, embarked on their "education" very early indeed—just as soon as they closed their tiny mouths, opened their beautiful eyes, and realized that they actually existed. They were here!

"Education" is by no means confined to the classroom or the lecture hall. It does not begin with preschool, kindergarten, or even lullabies and bedtime stories.

It begins long before that—just as soon as the "newcomer" is capable of absorbing (not learning, which involves a conscious effort) an experience, a recognized contact with the world outside of himself.

My eldest/youngest son (he, although my firstborn, never attained chronological maturity), following a particularly concentrated course in life experiences, "graduated," I would venture to say, "with honors" just before he got to 4 years of age.

In those less than four years Ady had "absorbed" a great deal, and I, in turn, had absorbed a great deal more from observing and interacting with him, closely and intimately, until his "graduation day," when he went to sleep to await his Savior's "wake-up" call: "School's in session again. Rise and shine!"

I spent all of my adult life, except for the years of World War II, involved with children, young people, and older people in a variety of "educational" settings. By the grace of God I was called, I believe by the Holy Spirit, to a lifetime of involvement in what Ellen White termed "the nicest work." She had it right.

During more than a half century I have had the inestimable privilege and honor of standing before or sitting on the floor with them, even having one of the tiniest ones on my lap, infinitely precious, impossibly beautiful, "lambs" belonging to the "beautiful flock" for which our Father holds us responsible.

I have "taught" (shared with) "lambs" ranging from tiny, often timid, first graders to "sophisticated," world-weary (sometimes) graduate students, and beyond. They are all, I have observed, although fascinatingly different from each other, very similar in that they all, whether 5 years old or 50, are really looking for the same elusive emotional "pot of gold" that, tragically, eludes so many.

Each of them, whether in "pigtails" (braids) or with a super-sophisticated "hairdo," long for, desperately need, and seek, sometimes unknowingly, acceptance. They long to be recognized as worthwhile, valued, respected, cherished individuals, as beautiful in their own right.

I realized very quickly that the words "teacher," "professor," and "pupil" or "student" are misnomers. I recognize, humbly and happily, that in all of my 50-plus years, I have never "taught" anybody anything. I have "shared" with them, and they, if and when they were ready, absorbed and accepted, or rejected, what I presented to them. And I, in turn, "learned" (absorbed) what they were, in turn, anxious to share with me.

I have often thought that, something like medical doctors and other health workers, we so-called teachers should be required to adhere to some sort of "Hippocratic oath," you recall: "First, do no harm."

Remembering, and being reminded each time I prepared to face a class, the precept from the Song of Solomon that "our vines have tender grapes" (2:15), I never entered a classroom without first imploring the children's Savior: "Dear Jesus, don't let me make anybody cry today."

Everyone, and children in particular, long for, above all else, a listening ear. They desperately need for their thoughts, their concerns, their hopes and fears, to be taken seriously.

Our Lord was a very good listener. In the account of His earthly ministry, we don't read a great deal of what He said. We read often of how He introduced Himself to someone who crossed His path, maybe asked a question, then listened to what was on the mind or the heart of the one He had come to save.

In addition to formal "teaching," I assisted for 35 years in the Primary Sabbath school room. The wise, caring woman in charge of the room assigned me to "welcoming" the children as they arrived. I welcomed each child by name, most often gave them a hug if they were receptive (most were), and pinned their felt name tags onto their clothing. They looked for this, and it meant more to them than the mere identification process. They had been recognized and accepted for who they were. They didn't put it into words, but their smiles and their shining eyes said, very clearly, "I'm here. I'm recognized. I'm me!"

I loved those kids. Every one of them.

One, in particular, comes to mind: Sammy (not his name) was a little African-American boy from a children's foster home in the village near the church I attended. Sammy was a charmer. Sammy, today, would have been diagnosed as a child suffering from attention deficit disorder. He just could not sit still for more than a few minutes. Then he would spring up off his seat and flit around the room like a will-o'-the-wisp.

The other children, "accepting," as most children are, were not put off by Sammy's behavior. No big deal. It's OK. This is Sammy.

One "primitive" therapy, though, was effective (sort of), at least for a few minutes. I was assigned to sit, on a child's chair, behind Sammy and place my hands gently on his slender shoulders, not restraining him, just touching him. This seemed to calm him, and he would sit quietly for sometimes as long as 20 minutes before resuming his—actually rather charming—flight around the room.

One time, soon after we had "settled in," I was interrupted by a visiting adult with a question and thoughtlessly took my hands from their place on Sammy's shoulders. The visitor left, and I turned back to Sammy, who, to my surprise, still sat there but with tears in his eyes.

"Oh, Sammy, whatever's the matter?" I asked him, replacing my hands on those tiny, vulnerable shoulders.

I still remember the stricken look on precious little Sammy's face. He looked at me, more sadly than accusingly. "You weren't holding me," he said.

Thank You, Jesus, for the precious, beautiful privilege of "holding" so many of Your "little ones" of all ages, in an effort, by Your grace, to reflect Your love and caring, however dimly, to the "lambs" and the older ones of Your most beautiful flock.

I have been blessed.

Chapter 25

How to Love Him

It wasn't really very far, but all the same, it seemed farther than she had thought it would be. Besides, she wasn't used to walking, especially not to a party. She could have easily afforded not to walk, except that she had spent all of her available money on the gift.

She shivered a little, not because she was cold, but in anticipation— or maybe it was apprehension.

She had been to many parties in her time. She couldn't begin to remember them all. Some of them had been given in her honor. She smiled at the thought. Although she was—or had been—a proud woman, *honor* was not a term she often associated with herself. Certainly at this party she was not to be the guest of honor. In point of fact, she hadn't really been invited. To put it bluntly, she had fully intended to be a gate-crasher.

She checked again to see if the gift was still safe. It was getting to be dusk by this time, and a few passersby—especially men—glanced curiously in her direction as she hurried along. She was used to being looked at, especially by men. She didn't mind it. In fact, she rather enjoyed their admiration. Indeed, in her business, when men stopped looking at you, you were no longer in business.

She was attractive, she knew. It was the red hair, she had no doubt. She had the sort of glorious red-gold hair that almost everyone looked at twice—enviously or resentfully if they were women, admiringly or lasciviously if they were men. It was very long—almost to her waist—and she devoted a great deal of her time to caring for it. After all, it had been her stock-in-trade, you might say, and when it was freshly washed and brushed, as now, it really was a sight to behold—like a river of spun gold.

She had known lots of men—many briefly, few intimately. Most she had despised, some she had pitied, a few she had hated.

But this man . . . she had never met any man quite like him before. There was an indefinable quality about him she couldn't quite classify. She regarded herself as something of an authority on men, but this man didn't seem to fit into any category with which she was familiar—and she thought her experiences had covered them all.

To be truthful, she didn't really know him that well. She certainly hadn't met him in a professional capacity. But in spite of their relatively brief acquaintance, she had a strange feeling that even if she didn't know him very well, he certainly knew everything there was to know about her.

She blushed at the thought. Yet if he really did know all about her, strangely she didn't really mind. She was somehow ashamed and proud and glad and sorry all at the same time.

She hadn't really thought he would ever speak to her anyway, nor had any of her friends—or her enemies. But he had spoken to her. Not very long ago, yet it seemed like two lifetimes. And she had thought of little else since. It seemed almost that there never was a time she hadn't known him. Although, certainly, her life had been very different since then. Yes, it really did seem to be two lifetimes—before she had met him and after she had met him.

She slackened her pace as she approached the house where the party was to take place. Should she go ahead with her intention or not? She didn't usually lack courage, but somehow she sensed that this was to be a turning point in her life.

It wasn't the house that intimidated her, big and luxuriously appointed though it was. She had entered many houses just as big and luxurious over the years. It wasn't the thought of meeting her "host"—if that was the right term when you were gate-crashing a party. She didn't intend to let him see her anyway.

No, she had to pause and summon up enough courage to approach the man again—uninvited. She wasn't sure that she could meet his eyes. His gaze was so penetrating and yet at the same time infinitely compassionate. She couldn't rid herself of this extraordinary conviction that he knew everything there was to know about her, although she had exchanged only a few words with him.

She heard footsteps behind her on the street. She must not be seen loitering here—not now.

Taking a deep breath and unconsciously smoothing her halo of red-gold hair, she walked up to the gate and knocked.

The servant who appeared in answer to her summons looked surprised to see her. He recognized her, of course, and opened the gate for her to pass through. Once she was inside, it was easy to get lost in the crowd of expensively dressed guests who were milling around, talking and laughing. There was music in the background and the clink of crystal from the long table loaded with refreshments toward the back of the beautifully furnished room. She had to hand it to her "host," she thought, momentarily amused; he did have good taste—in all kinds of areas.

She adjusted her gown and began to search through the crowd for the one she had come to see. She had devoted a lot of thought to what she would wear tonight. Finally, from her extensive—and expensive—wardrobe, she had selected a long, shimmering gown of deep blue, caught at the waist with a golden girdle. The girdle was almost exactly the color of her hair. She had told herself that she had chosen this particular gown because it was becoming yet not conspicuous. But in her heart she knew that this was not the real reason for her choice—or, at any rate, not the whole reason.

She had chosen it because it was the gown she had been wearing when she had first met him. She didn't know what he had thought of it. He had made no comment—an unusual experience for her. Most men were concerned with little else than her appearance. They didn't seem to realize that she had a mind like everyone else—better than many—and feelings. Oh, yes, she had feelings.

But he had known. Perhaps that was why she had been irresistibly attracted to him. Because, although he hadn't exactly put it into words, she had known that to him she was a person, a real, whole, living, thinking, feeling, and yes, suffering, almost despairing person.

Ah, there he was, off in a quiet, secluded corner of the room, talking to a couple of men. She had seen these fellows with him before—some of his friends, no doubt. She wished they would break off their conversation and go and get some refreshments or something. She wanted just a moment with him—but it had to be alone.

One of the servants appeared and made what seemed to be an announcement that she couldn't hear in the general confusion of conversation. The two men left him, and the guests began to drift over toward the long table, talking and laughing as they went.

It was now or never. She hurried across the room and knelt on the floor in front of him, heedless of her gown. He looked down at her, and she forgot all about the others in the room. For just that moment they were alone. He didn't speak. He seemed to have been expecting her.

Hurriedly she took the small package from the fold of her gown where she had concealed it. She broke open the box, and the tears that had filled her eyes and stood upon her lashes overflowed and ran down her cheeks like rain onto his feet.

It was only for a moment. Then the voices she had been anticipating, fearing, dreading, began. Angry, derisive, contemptuous voices. Leveling the most terrible of accusations at her, which, alas, were for the most part quite true. She bowed her head in an agony of shame and despair and tried to hide her face in her long, flowing hair.

Then he spoke. He spoke in loud, clear tones so that everyone in the huge room could hear his voice. It was very quiet.

"Leave her alone," he commanded. "She has done what she could (Mark 14:6, 8, NLT).

Chapter 26

Four Words for Jairus

Through the blinding glare of the day, through the dusty crowd, he forces his way along the narrow street. This is no time to stand on his dignity. He must find the great Healer somehow—it's the only chance. Everything else has been tried. She cannot—she must not—die. She is his only child, and she is too young.

Ah, there He is. He can see Him now by the seashore, talking to the people. But the crowd is too great. He cannot approach Him close enough to make his request. Finally, catching up with Jesus at the house of Levi-Matthew, his grief and anxiety overcoming his natural pride and arrogance, and heedless of the costly robes denoting his high position, the ruler of the synagogue falls at the feet of the Savior and pours out his story.

The words tumble from his lips: "My little daughter is dying. Please come and lay your hands on her; heal her so she can live" (Mark 5:23, NLT).

There were not many things that could have touched the heart of this arrogant ruler of the synagogue. Possibly this was the only way in which his proud heart could be softened. His little daughter—the little sunshine in his life—lay dying. This Jesus must come and help her. He believed that He could. He dared not doubt—or his last hope would be gone.

And Jesus, the record says, went with him. No mention of a reply. No words of reassurance or comfort for the brokenhearted father. The record just says that He went with him.

To the anxious man, Jesus seems to be in no hurry. Why doesn't He make haste? Doesn't He care that she—his little star—is lying there at home dying? Even now she may be dead—and Jesus is wasting time talking to some old woman who has accosted Him in the babbling crowd.

While He is still speaking, a messenger from the ruler's house, breathless and distraught, speaks directly to the frantic father: "Your daughter is dead" (verse 35, NLT).

Four words spell the end of his world.

Then Jesus turns to the grief-stricken father and says, "Don't be afraid" (verse 36, NLT).

As they approach the ruler's house, the procession of mourners is gathering: the wailing servant woman with disheveled hair, the men with their clothing torn—all joining in loud, prolonged wailing.

Instead of commiserating with the mourners, Jesus rebukes them: "Why," He says, "all this commotion and weeping? The child isn't dead; she's only asleep" (verse 39, NLT). The cries turn to derision. They've already seen the body of the child lying on the bed in her dim room. What does He expect to gain by such foolish statements?

Jesus ignores them. With authority He dismisses everyone from the child's bedchamber except for the sorrowing parents and the three who are with Him. For a moment He looks down on the slender form lying there pale and still. His heart is rent with greater grief than the moans outside can encompass.

While the father and mother stand a little apart, their sobs arrested as they gaze, He approaches the bed.

Taking a small hand in His own, He speaks softly to her: "Little girl, get up" (verse 41, NLT).

She stirs and opens her eyes. She gets up from the bed. She walks—runs—to her father's arms.

Turning to the wondering parents, Jesus says, "She will be hungry. Give her something to eat."

Chapter 27

That Changed Everything

Then it was true—even though it couldn't be true. She was so young, so bewildered, and so afraid.

The slender girl threw herself upon her bed and—finally—surrendered to a fit of sobbing.

Eventually, exhausted, she slept. While she slept she dreamed—and a voice spoke to her: "Mary, do not be afraid . . ."

And that changed everything.

Perhaps the hardest part was telling Joseph. Deeply in love, they were soon to be married. How could she tell him? What would he say? Would she believe her?

"Joe, Joe dear." She pulled him down beside her on a big rock near the path where they were walking, hand in hand. "Joe, I have something—something very important—to tell you. I'm scared, and

I don't know how to begin, so please listen. Don't say anything until I have finished."

Joseph, a number of years older than Mary, squeezed her hand, smiled tenderly into her frightened face, and sat down beside her.

Although it really took only a few minutes for Mary to tell the man she loved about the incredible situation in which she suddenly found herself, it seemed to her as if it were the longest—certainly the most difficult—speech she had ever made.

Finally it was out. Joseph had neither stirred nor said a word, only put his arm protectively around her shoulders as, inevitably, she began to cry.

Usually these two chattered away happily when they were together, or sat, companionably silent, stealing glances at each other with admiring, loving eyes.

This silence, however, was different. Mary had said all she could say at the moment. She felt drained, exhausted, and desperately apprehensive. Joseph, clearly, was deep in thought. At this point, he, invariably in charge of a situation, didn't know what to say—or to think.

Eventually he looked up, gazing directly into Mary's still-wet eyes. He removed his arm from around her shoulders and took both of her hands in his own.

"I love you, Mary," he told her, and he too had tears in his eyes. "But this changes everything."

Later that evening Joseph, in turn, also fell into an exhausted sleep, worn out after hours of futile thought and soul-searching.

At some point during his dream (if that is what it was) Joseph too heard a voice—perhaps the same voice of which Mary had told—call his name. The message too was uncannily similar to the words Mary had recounted to him earlier.

"Joseph, do not be afraid . . ."

There was more, but Joseph was almost too excited to listen. It seemed an eternity until morning, when he could go and find Mary and tell her that he too had an almost-incredible story to tell. He could hardly wait to tell her that he loved her—that, no matter what, it was going to be all right.

"It's not going to be easy, you know," he warned his young betrothed as they sat together on the rock where, earlier, Mary had been desperately afraid they were going to say goodbye to each other forever. "No one's going to believe us. I'm not going to pretend that it's—that he's—well, that I am . . ."

She smiled up at him, momentarily more mature than he, as he struggled for words.

"I understand," she assured him, patting his hand in what she felt was a maternal sort of way. "Don't worry about that. It'll be all right. We'll have each other."

"I love you, Mary," said Joseph, taking her in his arms. "I always have and I always will."

Tears shone in Mary's eyes. She could not bear to think of what she would have done if he had been unable to believe her—if he had thrown her aside.

As expected, the next months were not easy. There was a lot of whispering—some of it intentionally audible whispering—and innuendo about young girls and old men, and about men who pluck their figs before they are ripe, and other gems of what passed for wit.

But as she had said, they had each other, and it seemed that their love for each other grew daily, along with the expected little one.

But, finally, after the longest months that Mary could recall in her young life, it was almost time. Mary, a little different appearing than she had been when she learned that her life was about to change forever, but, according to Joseph, still the dearest and most beautiful girl in the world, wanted nothing more than to curl up in a soft, warm place and wait.

But even that was denied them.

"What are we going to do, Joe?" Mary wailed. "It's such a long way. We have no place to stay, and it might be almost any day now, you know."

Joseph tried to be brave and responsible and to look as if he had everything under control. He looked at his young wife, noting the fear in her eyes and the tears trickling down her cheeks. She looked about 10 years old, and unbearably, heartbreakingly vulnerable. It nearly broke his heart.

He gathered her into his arms. "Sweetheart," he said, "we don't have any choice. The government says we have to go and register at this particular place, and no other will do. And we will have to meet the deadline, too. You know how they are. Would you sooner have the baby at a roadside inn or in a prison? Don't be afraid. I'll be with you, and God will take care of us."

Sniffling, Mary clung more tightly to him and looked up into his face. "You won't leave me, Joseph," she said, "will you?" And, with a hint of her usual mischievous humor: "I suppose I should call you Joseph now—now that we're an old married couple, and soon to be parents."

A couple of days later, hand in hand, as always (they had been accused, by some, of being joined at the wrist), they began their journey.

They went on, the three of them, toward Bethlehem.

And that changed everything.

Afterword

A rthur Amott Milward, 86, of Kennett Square, Pennsylvania, died on Wednesday, October 28, 2009. Arthur was born in Derby, England, on October 26, 1923. He served as a medic in World War II with the British Army and as a missionary in Kenya in the 1950s before emigrating to the United States with his family. A graduate of Newbold College, Arthur worked as a teacher and editor at Pacific Union College in California until his retirement.

He was an active member of his church; a compassionate neighbor; a devoted father, grandfather, and great-grandfather; and a committed friend. Arthur was preceded in death by his two sons, Adrian and Timothy. He is survived by friends and students throughout the United States and world, and by his loving family: his daughters, Veronica and Victoria; his six grandchildren, Allison, Jessica, Benjamin, Abraham, Amanda, and Ian; and his great-grandson, Alexander.

Arthur continued to write and publish true short stories until his death. His top-selling book, *I'll Hold You While It Hurts,* is available at www.adventistbookcenter.com or by calling 1-800-765-6955.